TW
Become
ONE

*An Orthodox
Christian Guide to
Engagement and Marriage*

FR. ANTONIOS KALDAS
& IRENI ATTIA

ANCIENT FAITH PUBLISHING
CHESTERTON, INDIANA

Published by:
Ancient Faith Publishing
A Division of Ancient Faith Ministries
P.O. Box 748
Chesterton, IN 46304

All Old Testament quotations, unless otherwise identified, are from
the Orthodox Study Bible, © 2008 by St. Athanasius Academy of
Orthodox Theology (published by Thomas Nelson, Inc., Nashville,
Tennessee) and are used by permission. New Testament quotations
are from the New King James Version of the Bible, © 1982 by Thomas
Nelson, Inc., and are used by permission.

ISBN: 978-1-944967-21-5

Printed in the United States of America

28 27 26 25 24 23 22   16 15 14 13 12 11 10 9 8 7 6 5 4 3

Contents

Preface

THIS BOOK GREW OUT OF A NUMBER OF SOURCES. It began as a section from the Year 12 *Coptic Orthodox Studies* textbook, *Understanding*, used in the Coptic Orthodox colleges in Australia. Some of the material came from a talk Fr. Antonios delivered at a youth meeting at Archangel Michael and St. Bishoy Church in 2007, while the role-play in Chapter Six is from a session run by Fr. Antonios for some years at the Coptic Orthodox Diocese of Sydney, *Marriage Preparation Day*. Much of the significant psychological and counseling material has come from Ireni's regular Relationship Seminars, which she has conducted for some years with the Archangel Michael and St. Bishoy parish, as well as from her work at St. Bishoy Coptic Orthodox College, her work with the congregations of the Coptic Orthodox parishes of Sydney, and of course her experience in her own private practice.

We thank Fr. John Behr for his generous advice and for sharing some difficult-to-find articles with us; Fr. Vassilios Papavassiliou for giving of his time so generously to help us understand the Eastern Orthodox wedding ceremony; Fr. Gabriel Yassa and Mario Ghobrial for revising the manuscript and providing much valuable and very practical advice; Katherine Hyde of Ancient Faith Publishing for patiently and gently guiding us through the editing process; and Dalia, Samuel, and Bethany Kaldas for many valuable discussions on some of the more complex and controversial issues covered in this book.

Ireni Attia
Fr. Antonios Kaldas

"But above all these things put on love,
which is the bond of perfection." (Col. 3:14)

We dedicate this book to the ones to whom
we are bound together as one
—Dalia Kaldas and Amgad Attia

Introduction

One becomes two.
Two become one.
One becomes two.
From two, one comes.
And we begin again.
One becomes two . . .

The Riddle of Life

This is the riddle of life.
Our lives are characterized by the constant interplay between the one and the many, between unity and plurality, between isolation and community. This interplay describes everything that is most important to us as human beings: our sense of ourselves, our relationships with others, and our relationship with God.

One becomes two.
The cycle begins when a lonely person seeks the comfort and security of companionship. We all need someone we can trust, someone we can love who will love us in return. We seek this not only to meet our own selfish needs but more importantly to fulfill our inbuilt need to give love to others, for this is how we are made: in the image of the God who is love. And so we seek out another person to whom we can dedicate our lives and give unconditionally, being loved in return in like manner.

Two become one.

When we find that person, we cement the bond of love through the holy "mystery," or sacrament, of Christian marriage. Here the Holy Spirit sanctifies the unification of two individuals into one, a frighteningly intimate transformation that mirrors and prepares us for our ultimate unity with God.

One becomes two.

God is generous and fruitful, and so are we when we live out this sacrificial love in marriage and share with God in the act of creating a new human life. As He made us to be individuals yet bonded by love, so the couple gives the gift of independent yet beloved life to the child born of them.

From two, one comes.

Parents who truly love their children do not seek selfishly to hang on to them forever but find no greater joy than to see them grow and flourish and develop their own independent personalities, finding their own unique paths in life. So has God loved each of us and bestowed upon us the ability to determine our own fate. The miracle of marriage is that it produces more images of the God of love who then go out into the world to seek the comfort and security of companionship. And so . . .

And we begin again . . .

The cycle repeats. The cycle of love and growth, of giving and becoming, of the one and the many, of unity and plurality—the cycle of divine love that mirrors the nature of the God who is love.

This is the riddle of life.

Marriage Today

This book is chiefly intended to be read by couples who are intending to wed, although it may be of use to those who are still some distance from taking such a step, as well as those who have been married for some years already. It is offered in the hope that, by better understanding what they are embarking upon, they will be better able to navigate their journey together and enjoy a more fulfilling experience.

We felt this book was needed because every day we see couples, young and old, who suffer so needlessly in their married relationships. None, as far as we know, go into marriage intending to harm their partners. But that is what people often end up doing, out of ignorance, and harm so easily turns into resentment, anger, and hatred.

Modern Western culture is dominated by the primacy of the individual over the role of that individual as part of a community. This has led to more self-centered attitudes in many facets of our personal lives, a trend that is surely at odds with the Christian Gospel's message of unselfish, unconditional love. For the Christian, the only true fulfillment of one's individuality lies in the voluntary, even joyful surrender of that individual self to God and to others on the altar of love. Yet Western society today, with its relentless emphasis on individual happiness, consumerism, and the obsessive need to protect us from infringing on each other's rights, has shifted the focus of modern life away from self-sacrifice and made words like "submission" and "surrender" almost dirty words.

This focus on the individual has had consequences for the health of our marriages. We can see this in the numbers. As society has changed, so have patterns of marriage and divorce.

According to the Australian Bureau of Statistics,[1] the number of marriages in Australia fell from 6.4 marriages per one thousand people in 1993 to 5.1 per one thousand in 2013. Perhaps as people become more self-focused they become less willing to commit their lives to another person in the complete way that marriage implies. In the same period, from 1993 to 2013, the percentage of weddings performed by religious celebrants dropped from 57.9% to 27.4%, while the percentage performed by civil celebrants rose from 42.1% to 72.5%, an indication of how Western culture is moving away from the religious underpinnings of marriage.

This is both good and bad. It is good in that people are no longer marrying simply because their parents and their society expect them to. Thankfully, long gone are the days when your parents chose your spouse for you, and you might have met him for the first time at the door of the church at your own wedding. To be sure, other societal factors made many of these marriages ultimately successful ones, but those other factors have long since disappeared. Today we rightly value the concept of freely choosing to love and marry one's spouse, just as God leaves us to freely choose to love and follow Him.

But this shift is also a bad thing, because it means that people are entering into marriage without access to its deeper spiritual and eternal meaning and are thus being severely shortchanged. In the Orthodox Christian view, this is sin in the ancient sense of the Greek word *hamartia*: missing the mark, as an archer's arrow might fly astray and miss the target. Losing the sense of the holiness of marriage is not something worthy of divine punishment but of profound sadness and pity. We are diminished as

---

1   Australian Bureau of Statistics, "3310.0—Marriages and Divorces, Australia, 2013," http://www.abs.gov.au/ausstats/abs@.nsf/mf/3310.0, April 2015.

individuals, as groups, and as a human race when we subtract the sacred from the image of divine love that is marriage.

A Holistic Approach

Interestingly, psychology today is finding that the things that make for a good marriage are basically the things that Christ taught: mutual respect, mutual self-sacrifice, unselfishness, humility, and, of course, unconditional love. To be a good spouse, all you really need to do is be a good Christian. And that is something we all, as Christians, have to do, whether we marry or not.

Psychology has taught us that the most influential factors that shape adult relationships begin in childhood. By and large, those who formed healthy, secure relationships in their childhood are those who are most likely to form healthy, secure relationships as adults. For Christians, the foundational securely attached relationship is the one we have with Christ. A person who has a healthy relationship with Christ is well placed to form a healthy, secure relationship in marriage. He is then able to bring into the marriage the mutual respect, mutual self-sacrifice, unselfishness, humility, and unconditional love required for its quality and survival.

In addition to this, research has found that the marriages that thrive are those in which couples embrace their differences, are aware of the words they use with each other, and have a healthy view of intimacy. Psychology, therefore, does not disagree with the biblical foundations of marriage. In fact, modern psychologists are conducting research and writing papers, articles, and books that affirm the need for the Christian virtues of honesty, love, forgiveness, and so on.

As you can see from the above, in this book we will attempt

to bring together material from a wide variety of sources—spiritual, theological, liturgical, medical, psychological, and social—to provide the reader with a holistic approach to marriage that "marries" the best of modern human knowledge with authentic, age-old Orthodox Christianity.

As Orthodox Christians, we reject the division of our lives into partitioned territories of the sacred and the profane, the religious and the secular. This false division leaves God out of our day-to-day lives, as if He were only to be found in church and in the place where we say our daily prayers, but not in the workplace or in the local shopping mall.

But God is everywhere, and we are happiest when we involve Him in *every* aspect of our lives. He is waiting for you in the aisle of the supermarket, in the traffic jam on the highway, and at the baby-changing table at three AM on a cold winter's morning. He is there, not only before the altar on your wedding day, but also in the reception hall afterward and in the bedroom after that. Everything we do in our lives is meant to be sacred, to be shared with Him and sanctified by Him, from the smallest detail to the most momentous and life-changing decision. He is sharing your life from the moment you are conceived until the moment you die and beyond. In that spirit, then, let us begin the great journey of marriage, the riddle of life.

Outline of This Book

We will begin in Chapter One by considering something few people think of deeply these days: What might you do to prepare yourself for marriage and family life *before* you even meet your partner? What can you do to make yourself more "marriageable," to make yourself a better gift to your future spouse and children?

From there, we move on in Chapter Two to some practical issues about how to go about finding the right person, how to work out whether you are suited for each other, and how to make a decision that is often quite frightening for many couples. It is, after all, a lifelong commitment, and one you don't want to get wrong!

In order to safely navigate through married life and get the most out of it, it is tremendously helpful to understand its nature and purpose and to share this vision with your partner. Chapter Three therefore explores the meaning of marriage in detail, explaining how marriage works best when harmonized with our Christian faith and practice.

Chapter Four gets down to the nitty-gritty of a lifelong marriage. How can a couple understand themselves and each other and communicate effectively? How can they relate to each other in positive ways rather than negative ones? And what are the inherent differences in the ways men and women think, feel, and deal with life? We spend years training formally for our jobs—it is worth investing a little time and training in the much more difficult task of marriage and family life.

Chapter Five addresses some sensitive topics that are often glossed over, although they can play a big role in some relationships: gender roles, intimacy and sexuality, contraception and abortion, and domestic violence and abuse.

The final chapter takes us into the beautiful world of the Orthodox wedding ceremony, full of rich symbolism and pregnant with meaning. We compare the Coptic and Greek wedding rites, their similarities and differences, to help readers better appreciate these beautiful rites and use them to begin their journey as husband and wife as they mean to continue it: as a life-affirming, joyful spiritual experience.

We understand that in today's world many couples are time-poor, so we have included a set of reflection questions at the end of each chapter that provides a kind of summary of the main points, as well as a stimulus for discussion between couples.

Whether you begin with these questions and use the main text to elaborate on specific issues, or whether you use the questions to review what you read in the main text, we strongly encourage couples to reflect on these questions *together*. There is nothing so beneficial as honest, thoughtful dialogue to open the lines of effective communication, create mutual understanding and respect, and bring about a healthy, sustainable relationship. We offer these questions for that purpose.

CHAPTER ONE

THE ONE

Marriageability

*Be diligent to present yourself approved to God, a
worker who does not need to be ashamed.*

(2 TIMOTHY 2:15)

*Let love be without hypocrisy. Abhor what is evil.
Cling to what is good. Be kindly affectionate to
one another with brotherly love, in honor giving
preference to one another; not lagging in diligence,
fervent in spirit, serving the Lord; rejoicing in
hope, patient in tribulation, continuing steadfastly
in prayer; distributing to the needs of the saints,
given to hospitality. Bless those who persecute you;
bless and do not curse. Rejoice with those who
rejoice, and weep with those who weep.*

(ROMANS 12:9–15)

*If we would judge ourselves, we would not be
judged.*

(1 CORINTHIANS 11:31)

Who You Are

Many people spend a good deal of their lives thinking about their life partner. They think long and deeply about the characteristics they are looking for in a spouse, about what is more and less important, what they would be content with and what they certainly could not stand. They put a lot of thought and effort into choosing the "right one."

Once they find this person, they put yet more effort into molding that one to their own needs and tastes, consciously or subconsciously. Such a person will work hard to educate his partner, to expose her to his friends and interests, to get her involved in his pre-existing life.

Sometimes this leads to disappointment, and people often see the reason for this disappointment as being the failure either to find the right one or to mold the partner into the right one. This brand of disappointment is sadly all too common in modern life and perhaps has been common throughout the history of marriage, although expressed in different ways. Nowadays, it is often expressed in depression and the breakdown of marriages.

While putting all this effort into finding and molding the right one, many people do also see the need to work hard on themselves in preparation for marriage. A young lady will invest barrow-loads of energy, time, and money into making herself physically beautiful, or working to develop a cute way of speaking or an attractive walk, to make herself an attractive prospect for the army of eligible young men. A young man will be equally diligent in building up his muscles and learning to talk or act with a sense of authority and control in order to make himself desirable to the army of eligible young women. Both genders today also work hard to establish themselves in a successful career and build themselves up financially in this effort to make themselves a "good catch."

Unfortunately, the skills and traits that may help a person to *find* and *attract* a suitable partner are not always the same skills and traits that one needs to *maintain* a marriage for a lifetime. That is a totally different skill set—and one to which very few people seem to give a lot of thought. So before we start talking about finding the right person, getting to know him, forming a relationship, getting engaged, and eventually getting married, we need to take a little detour down a very private lane and do a bit of self-examination.

The question we need to ask is, "Am I marriageable?" Before I think of what my prospective spouse has to offer to me, I need to ask what I have to offer—not in the superficial or material things, nor in the features that will attract her to me—but what I have to offer as a life partner, as a human being. This turns out to be a surprisingly complex question to answer. What is it that makes a person a good spouse?

To answer this question, you might think about your most direct experience of marriage so far: your own parents' marriage. We are far more influenced by what we *experience* than by what we are *taught*. We learn our patterns of behavior, our strategies for dealing with relationships and other people, when we are young—when we are dealing with our parents, our brothers and sisters, and our friends.

We learn from them habits of behavior—some good, some not so good. If a child grows up with parents whose chief method of problem solving is a long and loud shouting match, she is likely to find herself using the same method to solve problems with her husband. At the very least, she is more likely to be comfortable with such methods than is a boy who grew up never once having seen his parents speak an angry word to each other.

A man who was accustomed to solving problems with his sister by hitting her is more liable to solve problems with his wife the same way. He never had the chance to develop and become comfortable with any other strategy. When he finds himself under stress, the ingrained reflex habit often overshadows the rational, thinking mind.

The girl who kept the peace with her authoritarian parents by frequently lying to them is liable to try to maintain the peace of her marriage by frequently lying to her husband. Why should she change? How could she change?

Change isn't easy. Even those who detested their parents' habits may sadly end up imitating them, much to their own disappointment. It is hard to change when you have never had the new mode of behavior modeled for you. You simply don't know how. So whenever you are faced with the need to get on with life, to make a difficult situation bearable, you fall back on the old practiced coping strategies.

When we bring negative habits of behavior into our marriage relationships, they can become our natural patterns of behavior with our spouses. This can lead to serious problems and unhappy lives—seriously, deeply, and depressingly unhappy lives. Those caught in the cage of their own negative habits often feel worse because they feel trapped, because they can neither understand why things are so horrible nor see any way out of that horror. But this need not be the case.

Some of us are blessed with happy, calm homes in which to learn good habits, but others are not so fortunate. It is possible to change your mindset and habits—lots of people have done it before. But a few ingredients are required: the humility to acknowledge that change is needed; the desire, the motivation, and the courage to pursue that change relentlessly; and availing yourself of support and expert help when you need it. Above all, the grace of God working in our hearts and minds is the fuel that powers the change, a fuel that is always available in abundance for those who seek it.

In fact, becoming more marriageable is one facet of becoming a better Christian. The transformation we are talking about is in essence a type of *repentance*, that spiritual practice every Christian needs to pursue daily. What makes a person marriageable is what makes a person a good Christian, and vice versa.

This comes as no surprise. Marriage is a relationship with another human being in the grace and care of God. Replace "another human being" with "all human beings," and you have a pretty good description of what the life of the Christian is all about. In a way, marriage acts like a magnifying glass, focusing our general relationships of love into one very intense relationship. Even before you marry, even before you meet your partner, if you are motivated to make yourself more marriageable, you are also motivated to make yourself a better person and a better Christian.

We can find the kinds of things you need to be marriageable in the famous Bible passages that speak of the things you need to do to be a true Christian (of course, we spend our lives striving to live up to these ideals). Here are a few examples. As you read them, think about how they would apply within an engagement or a marriage.

> Love suffers long *and* is kind; love does not envy; love does not parade itself, is not puffed up; does not behave rudely, does not seek its own, is not provoked, thinks no evil; does not rejoice in iniquity, but rejoices in the truth; bears all things, believes all things, hopes all things, endures all things. Love never fails. (1 Cor. 13:4–8)

Now the works of the flesh are evident, which are: adultery, fornication, uncleanness, lewdness, idolatry, sorcery, hatred, contentions, jealousies, outbursts of wrath, selfish ambitions, dissensions, heresies, envy, murders, drunkenness, revelries, and the like; of which I tell you beforehand, just as I also told *you* in time past, that those who practice such things will not inherit the kingdom of God.

But the fruit of the Spirit is love, joy, peace, longsuffering, kindness, goodness, faithfulness, gentleness, self-control. Against such there is no law. And those *who are* Christ's have crucified the flesh with its passions and desires. If we live in the Spirit, let us also walk in the Spirit. Let us not become conceited, provoking one another, envying one another. (Gal. 5:19–26)

You have heard that it was said, "An eye for an eye and a tooth for a tooth." But I tell you not to resist an evil person. But whoever slaps you on your right cheek, turn the other to him also. If anyone wants to sue you and take away your tunic, let him have *your* cloak also. And whoever compels you to go one mile, go with him two. Give to him who asks you, and from him who wants to borrow from you do not turn away.

You have heard that it was said, "You shall love your neighbor and hate your enemy." But I say to you, love your enemies, bless those who curse you, do good to those who hate you, and pray for those who spitefully use you and persecute you, that you may be sons of your Father in heaven; for He makes His sun rise on the evil and on the good, and sends rain on the just and on the unjust. (Matt. 5:38–45)

These are just a few of many passages on this theme.

It is not uncommon for Christians to make heroic and sincere efforts to practice this kind of Christlike life in their local parishes, and perhaps even in their workplaces and other public places, and then to feel that when they come home they can let their guard down. This means they treat their family members with much less kindness and courtesy than they would people outside the family.

In an engagement period, the couple are highly motivated to be on their best behavior with each other, usually with every intention of continuing that way. But once they are married and back into a routine of daily life, they drop their guard and relax their effort, and the bad old habits reestablish themselves, much to the couple's mutual disappointment. We encourage you, therefore, as you strive to make yourself more marriageable, to work on making permanent changes to your deepest character, not just superficial "Band-Aid" changes.

How to Change

Ideally, preparation for marriage would begin at birth. The way children are brought up through their infancy, childhood, adolescence, and early adulthood forms their personality, character, and habits. By the time you read this, it is almost certainly too late to do anything about that for yourself, but it may be something to keep in mind when you yourself become a parent one day.

The good news is that it is never too late to work on and improve yourself. So before you launch into the wonderful, wild adventure that is marriage, make your own marriageability one of your main concerns. Well before you are ready for marriage, well before you meet the right one, you will find a tremendous benefit in working to make yourself the kind of person who will indeed be a good husband or wife.

Let us turn now to the mechanics of this transformation. A critically important principle in spiritual life is that you can rarely change others, but you can always *change yourself.* Time and effort invested into making your partner into the person you want to be married to will yield little dividend, if any. But the same time and effort invested into molding *yourself* into the kind of person with whom your spouse will enjoy living returns a huge dividend. You really are the only one who can change you—no one else can do it. And your partner is the only one who can change himself—no one else can do it, including you.

A marriage where both partners are constantly disappointed with each other and blaming and criticizing each other will always be bitter, unsatisfying, and painful. A marriage where one partner is always blaming the other and the other partner is always blaming herself results in deep emotional and psychological problems, and no one is happy. But a marriage where each partner is willing to take responsibility for himself and is able to humbly work to change herself into a more pleasant spouse is a marriage that grows constantly in love and produces joy, peace, security, fulfillment, and contentment.

In marriage, this principle is one of the keys to success. In order for people to make lasting changes, they need first to be willing to entertain the idea that some things need to change. A person who responds to an expressed need from her partner by thinking or saying, "This is the way I am, and he just has to live with it," is resisting change. Even if such a person gives in and makes a change, it is likely to be only temporary. Honesty is therefore critical in any relationship, and it is something we need to cultivate well before we embark upon a marriage relationship. We need to learn how to be honest about what we are willing to work on and change (permanently) and what aspects of our character we are not willing to change.

Many young people do not find the right kind of motivation.

If you don't get into the habit of being self-critical (in a balanced way) and willing to humbly change yourself from your youth, what is going to magically change once you are married?

Of course, during the courting and engagement periods, you have a powerful incentive to be on your best behavior. You are attracted to this person, and you want her to be attracted to you, so you do everything you can, whether intentionally or subconsciously, to be the nicest person you can be.

But once you have won your spouse, once he is yours, that motivation is often diluted or even dissolves altogether. The desire to change and to be a good spouse only lasts when it comes from the sincere conviction that, marriage aside, it is our task in this life to become good people. Being marriageable is just one facet of this overall task, albeit one with serious consequences.

If transformation is to be truly effective, it needs to be *genuine*. The changes you make to your personality must not be superficial—they need to become a part of you. They can't just be something you do on weekends but must become built-in facets of your body and your mind. They have to be practiced and reinforced over and over until they come naturally.

Married life is like those crucibles used in the school science lab—the ingredients are sloshed together inside it, and the heat is turned right up. Living with someone else day and night makes it very hard to pretend. The real you is going to become obvious sooner or later. For some couples this revelation takes a long time, whereas for others it happens quickly. Either way, your spouse is, more likely than not, going to see through any insincerity.

Nor should you yourself settle for a life of insincerity. One of the reasons to marry is to have someone who knows me as I am, who sees the "real me" and who, because of this or perhaps even in spite of this, loves me. But must my partner simply put up with the unlovable parts of the "real me"? If the "real me" has unusually and obnoxiously smelly breath, wouldn't the kind thing be to invest some time in oral hygiene, rather than to make my spouse nauseated every time I come close? And surely the same thing goes for the "smelliness" in my heart, soul, and character.

True transformation requires *persistence.* Genuine change rarely happens overnight. Remember that you are gradually molding your very human personality, with all its complexities, nuances, inertia, and stubbornness. Much like weight loss, genuine, lasting change can't be achieved on demand or in a few days, and any changes you do achieve quickly are most likely going to disappear just as quickly. Lasting change takes patience and determined effort, together with the willingness to go back and try again and again when you fail.

This persistence itself is a sign not only of your love for your future spouse but also of your love for your eternal God, and even, in a way, for yourself. These changes make you a better Christian and a better human being. They are bringing you closer and closer to the ideal image of God you were created to be. They are fitting you for heaven.

The good news is that you are never alone in this journey. You have, of course, a loving God constantly watching over you, like a mother hen watching over her chicks. You have from Him the gift of the Mysteries (sacraments) of confession and communion to wipe away your tears and fill you with His love and His power constantly. You have loving people in your life who are willing to help guide you and support you. This network of support makes persistence so much more attainable.

Another area that has a huge bearing on how we prepare for marriage and choose our spouse is our *self-esteem.* People who have low self-esteem, or do not value themselves as they should, may find that they are willing to compromise their expectations of their potential spouse because they are happy that someone would even be interested in them in the first place. This can be a very dangerous situation in a marriage.

Similarly, a person with low self-esteem may be constantly looking for reassurance from her spouse, thus placing an undue emotional and psychological strain on the relationship. In order for a secure, healthy marriage relationship to be formed, it is critical that both partners have balanced views of themselves and of each other.

Even when we have identified those characteristics that indicate low self-esteem in a relationship, we may find it quite difficult to change them. For some, the difficulty stems from labels that were given to them in childhood, such as "You're lazy," or "You're so aggressive." Unfortunately, when we are labeled as children, we grow up thinking that the labels define who we are and who we must always be.

It is worth investing some time and energy into working out where our resistance to positive change comes from. We then need to change those ingrained beliefs about ourselves and replace them with a healthier set of beliefs about who we are. If you could see yourself through God's eyes, you would know what you were really created to be. You would then become empowered to change and to fulfill His vision for you, despite the hurdles.

When you have reflected on who you are, identified ways you could become more marriageable (and therefore a better Christian), and set in motion the process of lifelong change and improvement, you are ready to start thinking seriously about finding the right one. That is the theme of the next chapter.

Reflection Questions on Who You Are

» Why are the things that make you a good Christian the same things that make you marriageable?

» What characteristics would make a prospective partner more marriageable to you?

» Which of your characteristics do you think make you marriageable?

» Are there any significant differences between your answers to the last two questions? If so, why?

Reflection Questions on How to Change

» What is the difference between genuine, deep change and merely superficial and temporary change? How might you be able to tell them apart?

» What role does self-esteem play in our personal development, and why is it so important?

» In what directions would you like to develop as a person in the years to come?

» What are you doing to make this development happen?

CHAPTER TWO

ONE AND ONE

Engagement

He who finds a good wife finds benefits
And receives cheerfulness from God.

(PROVERBS 18:22)

Who will find a courageous wife?
For such a one is more valuable than precious
stones.

(PROVERBS 31:10)

Lord, You are aware that I do not know what is
good for me, and now that I am about to start
[this activity], how can I know if it is right unless
You guide me with Your grace? O Lord, I beseech
Your guidance in this matter; do not let me follow
my tendencies, lest I be confused and fall. Keep
me from slipping, help me and let it be according
to Your will. If You see fit, grant me Your blessing
to complete it. If not, remove this desire from my
heart. You know all things, and nothing is hidden
from You.

*Lord, I am Your servant; deal with me as You see
fit, since I realize that I will have neither success
nor peace unless I submit myself to the grace of
Your will. Teach me to say in every occasion, "Let
it be according to Your will, O Lord, not according
to mine." For Yours is the Kingdom, the power and
the glory forevermore, amen.*

(PRAYER FOR GOD'S GUIDANCE
BEFORE MAKING A DECISION,
COPTIC BOOK OF HOURS [AGPIA])

GETTING MARRIED IS ONE OF THE BIGGEST DECIsions a person can make in life. You are, for the rest of your life, forgoing the possibility of a certain kind of intimacy with every other human being on the planet and limiting yourself to the most intimate of relationships with just one person. It is a lifelong commitment that influences many other aspects of life, so it is worth doing all you can to make the right decision. In this chapter we will try to understand the nature and purpose of engagement so we can help you maximize your chances of navigating it safely and fruitfully and, ultimately, of making the right decision.

What Engagements Are For

Simply put, engagement is a period for finding out whether two people are suitable to marry one another. It sits in between that early period of socializing and perhaps dating, when two people discover each other and feel the first inklings of serious interest in each other, and the later period of marriage that follows the wedding. Unlike dating, engagement is a formal agreement that involves the couple and their families and is usually blessed by the Church.

Unlike marriage, an engagement may be broken without any feelings of guilt or regret—breaking an engagement simply means that the couple has discovered they are not suitable for each other. It is far better that they discover this before they enter into the serious mystery of marriage, rather than discovering it afterward and regretting the decision all their lives. We should never regret a broken engagement, nor should we think anything bad about the couple involved. It is almost certainly for the best.

During the engagement period, the couple gradually tries to get to know one another. There is always a strong temptation here to put on your best face, to be the nicest and most polite you can be. But it is important that you both try your best to be your true, authentic selves. This way, each of you gets to know the person you will actually be marrying, not some sanitized version.

Engagements work best when they are neither too short nor too long. Short engagements can lead to a hasty decision being made, since the couple did not have enough time to get to know one another well. This can lead to regrets and serious problems in later life. Excessively long engagements can also lead to problems, whether due to the stress of waiting too long, the growing pressure of physical temptations, or disagreements between the families, who are often keen to complete their parental responsibilities by getting their children married off and safe in their own homes. Generally, an engagement period of between one and two years seems to work best, although of course there may be considerable variation in this period due to particular circumstances.

Engagement at a distance presents a unique set of challenges. If you and your intended live in different countries or even different cities, the task of getting to know each other becomes even more complicated. The whole process may feel stilted and stuttering. Thankfully, in the technological age, the easy availability of email, phone calls, and video calling can alleviate some of these difficulties.

Nonetheless, there is no substitute for quality time together in person, and we consider trips to visit each other to be compulsory in order to give you at least some time to see each other in your natural habitats. You can learn so much about each other by going out with a group of friends, visiting the family home and observing interactions and relationships with parents and siblings, or even looking through each other's bookshelves. It has often been said, with some truth, that if you want to know what your intended wife will be like in thirty years, just look at her mother (or his father for your intended husband). This applies not only to physical appearance but also in some degree to attitudes, character, and personality.

The Five Stages of a Relationship

However long an engagement lasts and however it is conducted, the relationship is likely to pass through certain normal stages. There are five of these stages, and they tend to be evident in almost all relationships. Couples move through the different stages at different speeds and will move back and forth from one stage to another, but both partners will predominantly be in the same stage at the same time. These stages are not a linear process—they are more like a helix or spring, a circle spiraling upward. You retain stages and bring them forward as you grow— at any given time you are in one stage or another with bits of the others. Knowledge of the stages helps you to move through them.

The five stages are *romance, power struggle, stability, commitment,* and *co-creation.*[2]

Many couples meet, get engaged, and eventually marry while in the *romance* stage of the relationship. This stage satisfies a need for love and belonging in each person. It is characterized by its dreamlike qualities: fantasies, hopes for the future, possibilities, and the asking of the question, "What if?" Everything is wonderful, beautiful, fun, and exciting.

In this stage, the couple see reality through rose-colored glasses or through a fuzzy, out-of-focus camera lens. They keep their attention on the overall picture, while the details are obscure and specifics are not discussed. The couple are focused on similarities and do things to please each other. They view differences as bad, so they deny them. Each will do anything to get along. They deny parts of themselves, thinking, "Now that I have this other person, I am complete and happy."

This stage is short-lived, usually lasting from two months to two years, because you cannot be a whole person in this state. But the stage does allow for the building of a foundation for the relationship in the future. Romance allows one to take chances and risks; it nurtures a belief that "I can do it."

However, real love cannot begin at this stage—paradoxically, one must fall out of love in order to learn to truly love. Romance takes up a lot of energy, with all the courting, pretensions, and trying to be the same as your partner. Eventually you begin to tire. When the cost to your individuality becomes too great, you start trying to change the other person. The other resists, you try to insist, and there is a fight, leading to the next stage: the *power struggle.*

---

2   The five stages of relationship are compiled from *The Couple's Journey* by
     Dr. Susan M. Campbell (San Luis Obispo, CA: Impact Publishers Inc.,
     1984).

It is best that the power struggle stage take place prior to the *commitment* stage (that is, marriage), as it prepares you to navigate the difficult issues you will face and provides you with the opportunity to work out your differences. During the power struggle stage, the lens through which you view your partner and your relationship becomes a crystal-clear zoom lens, and you focus in on every minute detail. Indeed, your differences are magnified.

During this stage, you can learn both how to have healthy, robust discussions around matters you disagree about, and how to come to agreed solutions. You may realize that such solutions are not possible given your personalities, that your differences are too great for you to be able to have a successful marriage relationship. This is why it is best for a couple to experience this stage for the first time before they marry rather than after, when it will be too late.

The end product of this stage of a relationship is that you learn to be together out of choice, rather than out of need, as you were in the romance stage. This stage is necessary to make you ready to relate to each other as whole people. You need to see it as a positive phase in your relationship: an opportunity to journey together, to learn how to fight fairly with both of you coming out winners, and to embrace each other's individuality.

If you successfully navigate through the power struggle stage, you then move into a phase of *stability* in your relationship, where you have learned how to communicate through your differences and have accepted that you are not going to reshape each other. Stability means that you have learned mutual respect for each other, or else you will slip back again into the power struggle stage. Ideally you will reach the point of stability in your relationship prior to getting married.

You will then be ready for the *commitment* stage, where both individuals are wide awake, making clear choices about themselves and their partner based both on their differences and on what they have in common. You see, appreciate, and respect both your own needs and those of your partner and are willing to work together toward meeting them. You now choose each other with a fuller awareness of the past and present, as well as the direction of the future. The needs fulfilled here are a balance of love, belonging, fun, power, and freedom. You don't *need* each other; you *choose* to be with each other.

The *co-creation* stage is the final and continuing stage of a relationship. It is where the couple are able to continue to flourish in their relationship while being involved together in external projects. These can be such things as children, church services, or a business venture. It is important for a couple to continually nurture their relationship by setting aside time for each other as they grow their family or their projects.

It is important to emphasize that there is no escaping or detouring around these stages. A couple that marries after experiencing only the romance stage will still inevitably encounter the stages that follow. In fact, going through the power struggle stage for the first time after marriage places strain on a young relationship and is a common reason many marriages face difficulties in their early years. It is important to work through the earlier stages, honestly and with love, as far as is possible during the engagement period before you enter the stage of commitment.

We must emphasize once again that marriage is never a decision to be rushed. All parties concerned should take their time and do things right, seeking God's true will. If serious doubts remain, it is far better to delay a marriage, either until the doubts can be resolved or until it becomes clear that this marriage is not meant to be.

Spirituality during Engagement

Working your way through these stages together is not easy. We might almost say it is beyond human ability. You will need the grace of God in your lives. This grace will not only help you as you discover each other and negotiate the hills and valleys of such a close relationship, it will also help you to build the pattern of your future life together. The habits you develop as a couple during engagement are most likely the habits you will continue once married and, later, when you begin your own family.

Each of you needs to maintain your personal spiritual life with God, of course, but with guidance from your spiritual fathers, a joint spiritual practice should also be introduced. This may include praying together whenever you meet, reading the Bible and discussing it with each other, or even memorizing a passage from the Bible together (1 Cor. 13 is a popular one for engaged couples). It might mean attending liturgies and partaking of communion together, attending youth group or Bible study meetings together, and even serving others together.

A strong spiritual life will also serve to protect you from temptations, particularly of the physical nature. The physical intimacy you will share with your spouse is a holy and profoundly beautiful thing, not something to be cheapened and disrespected by allowing base lust to dominate it. Engagement is a period where you will gradually build a life of physical intimacy together. Do not rush this phase, but take your time and enjoy the journey.

How fast should the physical relationship progress? Every couple is different, but the general principle is that physical intimacy should progresss at a rate that is comfortable for both partners. Decide together how close you feel you should become before you get married, then spread the journey to that point out over the period of time leading up to your wedding day. In fact, it is wise to give yourselves a buffer zone just in case, setting the maximum prenuptial point of intimacy a little on the side of safety.

Remember that physical intimacy is just one way you are learning to express your love and commitment to each other. Do not allow it to overshadow the rest of your relationship. The last thing you want is to develop subconscious feelings of guilt and self-hatred, or of resentment toward your partner for pushing you further than you were comfortable with. Think of the long term, develop healthy attitudes and habits with regard to intimacy, and remember that you will very likely have a good sixty-plus years to enjoy each other's company in the future.

Some couples like to involve their spiritual fathers, through confession or counseling, to help them to be accountable for maintaining reasonable limits of physical interaction with one another during the period of engagement. This kind of accountability can be very effective in keeping you on the right path.

Keep in mind that until the last moment before marriage, an engagement can be broken, so maintaining one's purity is very important. While physical intimacy is a holy and blessed expression of the love and unity between husband and wife after marriage, before marriage excessive physical interaction is not only a sin, damaging your relationship with God, but it may also seriously cloud your judgment about whether you are right for each other.

Physical attraction is a little like an intoxicating drug. It releases chemicals in your brain that have a powerful effect on how you think, feel, and behave. This kind of influence can conceal the fact that your personalities are not compatible with each other and that you can't really get along. Once you are married and the urgency of physical desire dies down, you may sadly discover that you are stuck with the wrong person. It is far wiser to keep your mind as unclouded by desire as possible during the period of engagement.

Compatibility

The approach we suggest to discovering whether you and your partner are compatible may seem a little too logical or too hard-headed for some. We are not at all denying the importance of emotions and of romantic love for each other, but we are suggesting that such emotions alone may not be the best foundation for a lifelong relationship. In fact, if they are very strong emotions, they may even make you both blind to some very serious ways in which you are not a good fit for each other.

Of course, by their nature, strong emotions cannot last forever, like a roaring fire that soon burns away all its fuel and dies out. Once this has happened, if there is nothing else keeping you together, the relationship will begin to feel like a prison. It is therefore important to give serious thought to whether you and your partner are compatible.

But what does this actually mean? We need to introduce two important concepts before getting down to the nitty-gritty of how to find out if you are compatible with someone. The first one is what a "successful marriage" means, and the second is what "compatibility" itself means.

First, what makes a marriage successful? We don't believe there is a single answer to this question that applies to every couple. As you work your way through the discussion of compatibility below, you will realize (if you haven't already) that success in life means different things to different people. Because each of us has a unique personality, each of us also feels successful in different circumstances. For some, achieving goals in their career is paramount; for others, being a good, kind, and decent person, regardless of career success, is all they need.

You need to think carefully about what success in marriage means to you and what it means to your partner and find out whether the ways you define success in marriage fit together well or not. One way of doing this is to ask how you would ideally like to see yourselves in, say, fifty years' time. When you reach that age together and look back at your married life, what are the things that will make you say, "Ah, now that was a great marriage!"

From a Christian point of view, of course, there are certain things one would hope would characterize those fifty years of marriage, such as unconditional love, humility, unity, honesty, and so on. These things not only mean that you have a good marriage but also that you are a true Christian. We will return to these things in Chapter Four. But you must also ask yourselves about the specific things you as individuals care about, dream about, and hope for in a marriage.

Those general Christian characteristics of a successful marriage also tell us something important about the nature of compatibility, the second important underlying concept. In today's romance-soaked media, there is a prevalent subconscious conviction that everybody in this world has just one special person with whom they are meant to be for the rest of their lives. Tear-jerking movies feature two people fighting against the world, overcoming all odds to find their perfect match. So let us be quite clear that we are in no way suggesting here that, of all the people in the world, only one partner exists with whom you can have a long and happy marriage.

The reality is that there are probably many people in this world with whom you could have a happy, enduring marriage. Some people are not very flexible in their character and their relation-ships, and there may be only a few people with whom they can forge such a relationship. Other people are far more flexible and could have a happy marriage with any one of thousands, perhaps tens of thousands, of prospective partners. So when we speak of compatibility, we are not saying, "This is how you find that *one* special person with whom you can have a successful marriage." Rather, we are saying, "This is how you find another person with whom, more than most other people, you can share your life and have a successful marriage."

Why are these important concepts to think about? Because some people spend their whole lives looking for that "one special perfect person" and never find a spouse, much to their unneces-sary disappointment and lasting loneliness. We would like to help you avoid that fate. Besides, having that idyllic, romantic view of your partner is sometimes just asking too much of a frail and flawed human being, not to mention the relationship between two such frail and flawed human beings. Holding that kind of idealistic view may be setting you up for failure—striving for a fantasy that can never exist in this fallen world. This can only end in bitterness and disillusionment.

Neither is this romantic ideal of "one special perfect person" a part of the Christian view of marriage. In fact, if marriage is about practicing Christlike love, then it involves loving someone in precisely those moments when he is least lovable, sticking by someone when you get nothing out of it, and finding and embrac-ing the beauty in someone when she is at her ugliest. Marriage is about giving yourself to your spouse *in spite* of your imperfec-tions, and becoming a better person—and a better Christian—through that self-sacrificial giving. This is a difficult thing to do, as difficult (and as necessary) as learning to breathe for yourself at the moment of your birth. Our discussion about compatibility below is aimed at helping you do all you can to enter into this difficult process with the cards stacked in your favor, rather than against you.

Let's get down to the nuts and bolts of how to work out whether you and your partner are compatible. The first point to note is that as a Christian couple, you are not working in isolation. His Grace Bishop Moussa, the Coptic Orthodox Bishop for Youth, distills his long experience in counseling young couples into a succinct and surprisingly effective formula:

» Pray a lot.
» Think a lot.
» Feel a little.
» Seek spiritual guidance.

By choosing to make prayer your first step toward making a decision, you are consciously putting God's will first, above your human will. This is just what we pray every day in the Lord's Prayer: "Thy will be done on earth as it is in heaven." As Christians, we understand that we are limited in our wisdom and that we cannot see all factors. None of us can see inside the deepest and most secret places of another person's heart. There is unavoidably an act of faith involved in committing your life into the hands of another person as fully as you will in marriage. You certainly will want to make such a major decision in cooperation with God, seeking His wisdom as well as His blessing.

This is one example of the Orthodox Christian concept of *synergy*, the idea that our lives are meant to be conducted not through our will alone, nor through blind submission to God's will alone, but through a relationship of cooperating together.

Of course, it is only out of God's immense love for us that He deigns to call us partners, for there is a great gulf between our nature and His. His contribution to the project is His love, wisdom, and grace. Our contribution is our love, effort, and surrender.

Knowing that your choice of spouse is blessed by God is not only comforting as you make the decision to marry but also a great strength and support for the rest of your married life. When things get tough, as they are bound to in every marriage at some time or other, you can always fall back on the knowledge that this is the person God wants you to be with. This provides you with the confidence to be patient and persistent and to work through problems to their happy resolution.

We will skip past the second step for now, as the rest of the section is dedicated to discussing it.

The third step, "feel a *little*," is a reminder of the fickleness of pure emotions. An approach to marriage that allows the head to rule the heart tends to be more successful than one that works the other way around.

The fourth step, seeking spiritual guidance, reminds us that often the confession father or spiritual guide can provide an objective third-party perspective, which is especially valuable coming from someone who knows you well. This step most certainly does *not* mean that your spiritual guide ought to make the decision for you. It is you who must live with the decision, not he! But there is no doubt that, in most cases, a sensible spiritual guide who has your interests at heart can provide a much-needed sounding board.

The second step of the recipe, "think a lot," is the one that needs the most effort. As you get to know each other better, you need to think about whether you are compatible. Compatibility means that your personalities work well together, that you complement each other and fill what the other lacks, and that you make each other happy.

For a successful lifelong relationship, a married couple needs to be compatible in many areas, not just one or two. For example, a couple who strongly share a common interest (for example, they are both Olympic athletes) but who cannot have a peaceful discussion together for longer than five minutes are unlikely to enjoy a happy and fulfilling relationship.

Positive compatibility is where you have common interests, goals, and attitudes. This will help greatly in bonding you together as a single unit, a team working together to pull in the same direction.

It is important to note that "compatible" does not mean "identical." Some of your individual characteristics might be identical, but some might be quite different or even directly opposite. Differences, however, can *complement* each other—salt and pepper taste utterly different, yet they complement each other beautifully.

But *negative compatibility* is just as important. This means working out whether you can put up with the bad things in each other. We have often urged engaged couples to think of what is worst about their partners—an unusual occupation for a Christian! But you *must* know the worst of what you are getting yourself into. If you are confident that you know the worst, and you are happy to live with it, then you are onto a pretty good thing. If, on the other hand, that worst thing is a deal-breaker for you, then maybe it is better to rethink the relationship.

An important principle that cannot be stressed strongly enough is that when you marry, you should not *expect* your spouse to change. You must be willing to live with your partner as he is today, for the rest of your lives. If she has any faults today, you need to be fully willing to accept her, faults and all. You may hope that your partner will change—you may even work to help him change (with his full cooperation, of course)—but on no account should you make the success of your marriage in any way dependent on her changing. You must be willing and happy to take your partner as she is for the rest of your lives. After all, she also has to take you as you are. To begin your lifelong relationship by putting pressure on your partner to improve is unlikely to contribute to the cultivation of a healthy relationship.

By the same token, it's also important to understand that people do tend to change over time, and often not in the direction you wanted. Your partner cannot be the same at forty-five as she was at twenty-five. Life, responsibilities, and stress cause people to change and adapt, depending on their circumstances. It's important to be flexible and not expect that your future spouse will have, throughout the life of the relationship, the same characteristics, physical appearance, and priorities he had when you first met. Adaptability is a key aspect of a healthy relationship.

Of course, this in no way cancels our responsibility as Christians to grow, progress, improve, and repent. But, as we observed above, the only person in the world you can truly change is yourself. This does not stop you from being a good influence on each other—indeed, that is what we hope for. But the crucial point to emphasize here is that there is no guarantee that the change you want in your partner will happen. If you have set your heart on such change happening, and it doesn't, then you are setting yourself up for disappointment and bitterness.

How can you know if you are compatible with your partner? Most people just go on their feelings or intuitions. If it feels right, if it seems that we are getting along pretty well, then we must be compatible. Feelings and intuitions are a reasonable guide to life in many situations, but they can also get things terribly wrong. For such a major decision with such serious consequences, it may be wise to add a little cold, hard thinking, as Bishop Moussa suggests.

To help you do this, we have listed below a number of areas of compatibility through which you can better understand your respective personalities and their relation to each other. The idea is to read through this list and discuss each item together, as honestly and openly as possible. Remember that you do not need to have the *same* answers to every question, but you will hopefully have *compatible* or *complementary* answers. Two people who think and behave in exactly the same ways are likely to have a somewhat boring life. Variety is a good thing in that it opens our minds to seeing the world in new and wonderful ways. But if your answers are directly contradictory and your discussion of them together suggests that you cannot see the sense in the other person's point of view, that should ring some alarm bells.

The seven areas of compatibility we shall look at are *spiritual, moral, social, educational, emotional, physical,* and *financial or material.*

Spiritual Compatibility

As you spend time together, you will find out if you have the same understanding of God. Marriage is the most intimate, honest, and therefore vulnerable relationship you will ever have in your life. It is, in the eyes of the Church, first and foremost a spiritual union between two people, giving themselves body, mind, heart, and soul to each other, in a glorious image of the divine love that unites us with Christ Himself and fits us for heaven. Finding someone who is spiritually compatible may not seem critically important in the short term, when things like physical attraction and the spell of romance may dominate your feelings about the relationship. But if we see marriage as a lifelong partnership that must weather all sorts of storms and fit us for eternity with God, spiritual compatibility emerges clearly as a crucial factor.

On a day-to-day level too, many practical problems arise when partners are on different spiritual wavelengths. For example, a husband may become jealous of his wife for spending too much time at church, feeling that he should have the right to that time. Or a wife may get angry with her husband for continuing to pay his tithes during a period when money is a little bit tight. Problems can also occur when one person believes he is on a higher "spiritual level" than the other, thinking this gives him the right to preach at or rebuke the other partner for her spiritual slackness.

Marriages between people from different Christian churches have an added challenge, since the two partners will have been brought up with different approaches to faith. We sometimes see this kind of difficulty even when two people have been brought up in different parishes within the same church and in the same city! When one of the partners is from a non-Christian background, the differences are amplified even further. We will come back to the unique challenges posed by mixed marriages later.

Reflection Questions

» How do you relate to God? Do you see Him as Master, Judge, Father, or Friend (or some mixture thereof)?

» How much do you depend on God? Do you think He solves all your problems, or do you prefer the adage that "God helps those who help themselves"?

» Do you put God as your first priority in life, above all things?

» What role do you want God to play in your relationship with each other?

» What are your attitudes toward prayer, the Bible, going to liturgy early, and having confession and communion regularly?

» What are your attitudes to service in the Church and to giving tithes?

» How would you classify yourself religiously: conservative, moderate, or liberal?

» What is the role of the confession father or spiritual guide in your personal life? How involved do you expect him to be in your relationship?

» What do you see as your role in helping your spouse reach the Kingdom of heaven?

Moral Compatibility

Spiritual compatibility also becomes important when moral decisions arise. Such decisions are unavoidable in life, as you have no doubt already experienced as a single person. Once you are married, you can no longer make major moral decisions by yourself, for now they are likely to affect your partner just as much as they will affect you, and in many situations you may both be held jointly responsible. Eventually, they will also affect your children.

A significant proportion of our opinions of others derives from the kind of moral stands we see them taking. You will find yourself growing in your love and respect for your partner when he lives nobly, according to his principles, and losing love and respect when he acts meanly or selfishly. If you should choose to do something illegal or unethical, it is more than likely that your spouse will share the burden of feeling guilty with you.

Some moral decisions will have a great practical impact on your partner. For instance, a decision not to take a promotion because it would involve acting against your conscience means that both of you will have to forgo the additional income the promotion would have brought. So working out how you will handle moral decision-making together is a very important part of working out whether you are right for each other.

If you both hold your Christian beliefs, the Bible, and the Tradition of the Church to be the final sources of moral truth, then many problems that depend on individual opinions can be quickly resolved. For example, if one partner feels it necessary not to be completely honest in filling out his tax return, the other can appeal to the Christian principle of honesty.

Yet even this is not the all-purpose solution some take it to be. We must remember that two people who absolutely believe in following the teachings of Christ may yet *interpret* those teachings in different ways. One person emphasizes the verses that speak of God blessing those who fear Him with material success, while another emphasizes Christ's commandments to those who would follow Him to sell all they have. Both can claim to have the backing of the Bible behind their point of view. That is why it is important to talk through these issues openly and in detail together.

Reflection Questions

»   What do you think are the most important moral or ethical principles?

»   How strictly does each of you feel you need to adhere to moral or ethical principles? Are you very strict in your adherence to moral principles, or do you prefer a pragmatic approach: sometimes it is necessary to bend the rules in order to get on in life? What do you think of the principle that "the ends justify the means"?

»   What are your views on different areas of morality, such as

sexual, financial, environmental, and political morality?
» How much do things like world poverty or global warming bother you?
» It may be useful to discuss some hypothetical ethical dilemmas together to help you to understand each other's ethical and moral personalities. For example, if your partner was sick with a terminal disease and you could not afford the only available drug that could heal her, would you be justified in stealing that drug to save her life? Of course, such hypothetical situations are full of flaws and limitations, but they may help you understand each other a little better.

Social Compatibility

A married couple may need to learn how to vacuum, but they cannot live in a vacuum. You will inevitably interact with family, friends, neighbors, fellow parishioners, workmates, and strangers. Each of you has been brought up to deal with people in a certain way. If your ways are very different, this may cause problems. During engagement, you need to discover how your partner interacts with other people and find out if your respective styles fit together.

For example, different families have different expectations of how much time they ought to spend together. Will you be visiting your in-laws once a month or every evening? In some families, one member's problem is everybody's problem, and the whole family is actively involved in solving it. In other families, members tend to keep to themselves. You need to find out about each other's families, take the time to study the family dynamics in action, and come to understand them. Only then can you make a proper decision as to whether you can fit in.

You also need to know if you approach social situations in the same way. If one partner is very relaxed about social situations while the other is constantly worrying, one of two things will happen. Either there will be constant friction as you each consider the other to be either overreacting or underreacting, or else you will learn to appreciate each other's coping styles and benefit from the difference. Which of these happens will depend a lot on your respective personal abilities to be flexible and to accommodate and appreciate differences in others.

As time goes on and you grow older, it is important for you to have common interests that can keep you together, helping you maintain your sense of unity and of sharing your life together. Marriages where both partners are living in worlds of their own are heading for trouble. So at this early stage, it is important to work out if there is at least potential for developing common interests.

Reflection Questions

- » Do you have the same kind of friends?
- » How comfortable do you feel when you are in your partner's circle of friends?
- » How comfortable do you feel when you visit your partner's family?
- » What interests or hobbies do you share in common?
- » Do you have many topics of common interest that you talk about?
- » Are you the kind of person who thrives on being with others, or do you prefer to stay in and have a quiet evening?
- » How often do you feel you should visit parents or siblings?
- » How involved in your life do you want your friends, relatives, and in-laws to be?

» How much do you feel others should know about your lives?

Educational Compatibility

This is an area that used to be much more important in the past, but it still retains some relevance even in today's supposedly egalitarian and classless Western society. If the two of you are not on roughly the same intellectual level, the relationship may be an unbalanced one. This does not necessarily mean that it will fail, but it can place extra pressures on the relationship.

Although modern Western society is supposed to be classless, many people (especially in ethnic Orthodox Christian immigrant communities) do still think in terms of social classes: upper class, lower class, working class, and so on. Such class distinctions are often related to a person's educational level.

Consider the extreme situation of a couple where one is highly educated and intelligent and the other is poorly educated and of below-average intelligence. What sorts of problems might they face? The educated partner may be tempted to look down on the other, perhaps ignoring her input into discussions and decisions, and even putting her down at times. The less-educated partner may be tempted to feel inferior, lose his self-esteem, or develop resentment toward his spouse, who might seem arrogant and proud. Would they be embarrassed to introduce each other to their respective workmates?

To some people, class distinctions are important, while to others, they mean very little. If you are from different educational or class backgrounds, then you and your families need to work out how important education and class are to you and to what extent, if any, differences in these areas are likely to affect the relationship.

Reflection Questions

» How well do you get along with your partner's workmates and friends?

» How do you feel about your partner's abilities and achievements? Do you see them in a positive light, or do you see them as a disappointment or as a threat?

» What are your views on ambition? Is it something you admire, or something you consider harmful to your happiness and contentment with life?

» Would you support your partner if he or she wished to pursue further education after marriage, with all the sacrifices that might require from you?

Emotional Compatibility

Many girls are looking for a romantic Prince Charming who will ride up on a white horse and sweep them off their feet. In real life, successful marriages almost never begin with a white horse. It is worth emphasizing again that while a certain kind of emotional compatibility is important, the "butterflies in the stomach" emotion is not the *most* important thing. If nothing else, it is very hard to maintain over a long period of time, while marriages are meant to last for a lifetime. On the other hand, the more moderate affection that develops between two people who are truly compatible and live together for many decades just keeps growing and growing. This affection is perhaps closer to friendship than to romance.

You need, then, to have temperaments that are compatible with each other. Every person is a unique individual and has his or her own temperament: calm or volatile, talkative or quiet, introverted or extroverted, and so on. We also have our own love languages (see Chapter Five), our preferred ways of expressing and receiving love. This is one of the reasons the world is such an interesting place, and if viewed positively, our differences can make marriage a truly exciting adventure. A standard personality test like the Myers-Briggs scale may be of help here.[3] It can help you understand your own temperament, as well as that of your partner, and explain a lot of behaviors that may otherwise have puzzled you.

Again we find the principle of complementarity comes into play. A couple need not be identical in their temperaments, but they do need to be compatible or complementary. That is, they must be able to appreciate their temperamental differences and bring them to bear on each other in ways that enhance their lives, rather than letting them become a source of disagreement, disharmony, and discontentment. In addition to individual differences, as we will discuss later, men and women are intrinsically different in their emotional character. Each of you must understand this and make allowances.

Reflection Questions

» How important is romance to you? How important is it to your partner?

» What is your personality type, and what are the common problems that arise between this type and your partner's type?

» What is your preferred "love language"—physical touch, words of affirmation, quality time, giving gifts, or acts of service? What is your partner's?

» Do you prefer to confront problems head on and solve

---

3   For an excellent introduction to this topic, see David Keirsey and Marilyn Bates, *Please Understand Me* (Del Mar: Prometheus Nemesis Book Company, 1984).

them, to quietly and patiently find a compromise, or perhaps even to avoid them altogether and hope they will
go away?

» Are you hotheaded or calm and rational?
» Are you able to work out your problems together, or are you
constantly misunderstanding each other and seeing the
worst in each other?
» How do you deal with problems and failures?
» How much emotional support do you expect from each
other? What kinds of emotional support do you expect?
How much support are you able to actually give?
» Do you easily feel hurt, jealous, or proud, or look down on
yourself? What about other emotions?

Physical Compatibility

You will notice that we have placed this one fairly low on the list.
It is certainly important to choose someone with whose appearance you are comfortable—after all, you will have to look at him
or her every day for the rest of your life. There is nothing wrong
with marrying someone who is very good-looking, so long as you
are compatible in lots of other important ways. However, good
looks should be one of the last things on which you base your
decision.

St. Peter taught us that true beauty is not to be found in physical appearance but in "the hidden person of the heart, with the
incorruptible *beauty* of a gentle and quiet spirit, which is very
precious in the sight of God" (1 Pet. 3:4). We cannot choose
the kind of body we have or the bone structure of our faces,
but we can choose to be compassionate instead of selfish, noble
instead of cruel. It is our choices that really make us who we are.

Remember also that good looks never last. The day will

come when even the prettiest or most handsome of people will be frail, bent, toothless, and full of spots and wrinkles. Will you still love your partner then? Unfortunately, some marriages break up because they were formed on the basis of looks. In these cases, when the looks of one partner start to fade, the other partner sometimes divorces and looks for someone younger and nicer-looking. Other times, the dynamics of the relationship change, as one partner feels less attracted to the other and begins to treat her with less respect or kindness. Such behavior reveals an ugly shallowness of soul. As human beings we are far more than just the fleeting outward appearance of our bodies.

Reflection Questions
- » How important is physical appearance to you?
- » Do you have any major problems with your partner's appearance?
- » Do you ever catch yourself criticizing him, either silently or to others?
- » What level of grooming and dress sense do you expect from your partner? Are you comfortable with her expectations of you?
- » How much of your relationship would be preserved if you looked different?

Financial/Material Compatibility
Money matters appear on this list because, in practice, they cause a surprisingly high number of problems between married couples. We say it is surprising for two reasons. The first is that if you ask most people, especially Christians, whether they think they are likely to have a serious disagreement with their spouse over money matters, they will laugh with derision at the thought. The

second reason is that these kinds of problems are really not that hard to avoid. It only takes a modicum of healthy communication and mutual respect. Again, your approach to money and material things need not be identical to your partner's, but they must be compatible or complementary.

For example, in some families, one partner is extremely organized in budgeting and paying the bills, while the other just spends whatever money happens to be in his pocket that day. If the couple come to an agreement to let the organized partner look after the finances, they will probably live happily ever after. The organized partner will bring much-needed order into the other's life, while the more carefree partner will appreciate the extra spending power this order gives them. And the organized partner will in turn benefit from the excitement of the occasional splurge with the carefree partner that might otherwise never have happened. The two complete one another. On the other hand, if they are not capable of appreciating and respecting each other's approaches, then money will sadly become a source of constant bickering, judgment, and resentment between them.

It is also worth pointing out that some young couples today overcommit themselves financially at the beginning of their life together by buying a very expensive home or spending obscene amounts of money on their wedding festivities. This then puts a great deal of pressure on their lives and therefore on their marriage. They are forced to work long hours and to endure the stress of financial insecurity at a time when their married relationship is in a sensitive stage of formation. This danger too is something every couple needs to discuss and come to an agreement about before they commit to marriage.

Reflection Questions

 » How would you describe yourself: thrifty, a big spender, or somewhere in between?
 » How much do you worry about finances?
 » How important is it to plan ahead financially? Do you think a household budget is important? How strictly should such a budget be followed? What should happen when it isn't?
 » How do you feel about using credit? Is it better to borrow and pay later, or to save up first and then spend?
 » Do you have expensive or simple tastes in things like food, clothing, cars, houses, and so on?
 » What is your view of wives working full-time? What about mothers working full-time? House-husbands?
 » Are you willing to share the housework between you in order to allow both of you to work?
 » What is your attitude toward paying tithes and firstfruits, or making donations?
 » Will you put both your incomes into one account to be used by either? Will there be any ground rules to limit how the money is to be spent?
 » How much do you think it is reasonable to spend on a marriage celebration?
 » Do you plan to rent initially or to commit to buying your home?
 » When you come to buy a home, what portion of your joint income do you think it is reasonable to dedicate to your mortgage?

You will notice that there are some common threads running through all the areas above—concepts of complementarity, mutual understanding, respect, and appreciation. It is almost certain that you and your partner are going to be different in some ways at least. It is a good thing for you to be different. The key to turning those differences into pluses rather than minuses in your relationship is the attitude you each bring to bear on those differences. This is something we cannot emphasize too strongly.

The engagement period is not only a time of mutual discovery, it is also the time when you are laying down foundations for the rest of your life together. Habits you establish together now have a good chance of staying with you for the rest of your lives. If one of those habits is a positive attitude toward your differences, you will have gone a long way toward establishing a firm foundation for a happy and fulfilling lifelong relationship together.

The questions we have provided above do not cover all possibilities but merely some issues that we have seen commonly repeated across many relationships. Not all of them will be equally important to you. You may even have some questions of your own to add, relating to yourselves and your specific circumstances.

Having worked through the questions together with your partner, you will sooner or later come to a point where you feel you need to make a decision about whether this relationship should progress to marriage. Hopefully, this exercise will have placed you in a position where your decision can be much better informed and more likely to be the right one. But how does one go about actually making such a big decision?

Making the Right Decision

- » Pray a lot.
- » Think a lot.
- » Feel a little.
- » Seek spiritual guidance.

You will recognize Bishop Moussa's recipe. While there is of course no magic formula that will guarantee you the right decision, this recipe does distill for us the wisdom of experience, and it is worth following. Each individual person needs to find the way of making the decision that is most suitable for her personality and situation. However, we can elaborate on this simple recipe a little more. The suggestions below may be more or less useful to you, depending on your particular circumstances.

The Right Time

Don't start searching for your future spouse too early, before you're really mature enough and ready for commitment. As a general rule, you will still be developing your personality into your early twenties. This means that by making a lifelong commitment before that age you run a very significant risk of ending up in a relationship with someone from whom you grow apart as you complete your maturation. But don't leave it too late, either. If you are searching for a partner under the pressure of a ticking biological clock, you may feel you are being forced into accepting the wrong person for fear that your time is running out.

Prayer

As we mentioned above, prayer helps you work together in synergy with God, surrendering the matter to Him and truly seeking His will. Many Orthodox prayer books have some kind of formal prayer for those who have a major decision to make (consult your local parish priest). Praying with your partner on a regular basis also helps you to surrender the matter into God's hands together, inviting the Holy Spirit to be in your hearts, minds, and relationship as you make your decision. Some couples like to ask their parish priest to offer up the sacrifice of the Eucharist in their names or remember them at the altar.

Fasting

Some confession fathers recommend to their spiritual children to fast for a number of days as an expression that they are surrendering the decision into God's hands. It may be that, at the end of such a period of prayer and fasting, God's will becomes clearer in one way or another.

Get to Know Your Partner Really Well

Try to get to know what your partner is *really like*, not just what you *would like* him to be like. There is often a temptation to transfer the things you are looking for in a partner from inside your head onto how you see the actual person. Please resist this temptation if you want to avoid disappointment when reality hits later, after you are already married. As mentioned above, get to know the other in her natural habitat—at home, at work, with friends, and so on.

Of course, the other side of this coin is that you too should do all you can to be your real self around your partner so he can get to know you, warts and all. You may feel a sense of fear that if your partner gets to see who you *really* are, she might turn and run away. But in our experience, this almost never happens. Remember that your partner almost certainly has the same fears about himself. Good marriages happen between real people with real foibles and weaknesses. In this area of life, as in many others, honesty really is the best policy.

Take Advice and Take Your Time

We tend to take on board advice that agrees with what we already think while rejecting advice that goes against what we already think. This is just human nature. If people you trust and respect give you advice that you don't like, please don't ignore it! There are many sad tales of couples who insisted on marrying against the advice of parents, relatives, friends, and spiritual guides or confession fathers and later lived to regret it.

That is not to say that you should let other people make your major life decisions for you, but the fact is that your family and perhaps your closest friends are the people who know you best and love you most. If they see problems with your relationship, it is worth seriously considering their more detached points of view. They may not be right, but you owe it to yourself and to your partner to consider their thoughts as seriously and as honestly as possible. If there is any doubt, take your time—this is too important a decision to make without due deliberation.

Stick to the Rules

If you want God to help you make the right decision and to bless your marriage, then you have to create an atmosphere in which He is free to work. Engaged couples who introduce serious sins of any kind into their relationship (for example, lying, going behind parents' backs, sexual sins, greed, substance abuse, and so on) are basically telling God, "We don't want You here." Is that really how you want to live your life together?

No One Is Perfect

Those who wait until they find the perfect Mrs./Mr. Right will almost certainly remain single all their lives. We need to be realistic. A good rule of thumb is the one we mentioned earlier: think of all the worst things you know about your partner and ask yourself, "Can I happily live with *that* for the rest of my life?" If the answer is yes, then you have come one step closer to finding the right person. If, on the other hand, you realize that this person has that one human flaw that you simply cannot stand, then clearly this is not the person for you, however many other good things there may be in him.

In the end, marriage is an act of faith. There are no guarantees. But the Christian sees this very uncertainty as an opportunity to practice that unconditional and invincible divine love for which we were created and without which we are never truly fulfilled in life. Don't expect to find someone who is absolutely flawless. Strive instead to be as much as possible the perfect person for your partner by loving her unconditionally.

A Note on Mixed Marriages

The challenges that arise in a mixed marriage—that is, a marriage between people of different backgrounds or cultures—arise in addition to all the usual challenges we have discussed above. It can be very difficult to accommodate yourself not only to a new partner's personality and their family and friends, but also to a new culture, a new language, a new diet, a new parish, a new denomination, or even a new faith.

This is a situation that requires patience, compassion, understanding, and kindness from all sides. Marrying someone who comes from a different denomination or a different faith altogether does not just mean having lots of theological arguments. What we believe profoundly influences how we see the world, how we behave in that world, and how we treat others.

Our most cherished values are often based upon our faith. For example, the attitudes toward women that are prevalent in Muslim faith and culture differ significantly from those in modern Western Christian society. It is written indelibly in the Quran that the witness of one man is equivalent to that of two women, that a son inherits a double portion of his sister's inheritance, that the husband has the right to beat his wife when she is stubborn, and so on. Because these precepts are part of the Muslim faith and ingrained in the culture (even if they are not practiced fully), a man raised in that faith may feel a sense of betrayal of his identity should he neglect them, or perhaps be incapable of adopting other attitudes toward women. This is sadly not just a theoretical observation but one that we have seen in real life over and over again.

Similar if less serious differences arise when two people of different denominations marry, say, an Orthodox and a Protestant, or an Orthodox and a Catholic. Here the differences in belief, attitude, and practice are of course much smaller, and there will be a great deal more common ground on which both partners can stand together, but it still represents something of a trek outside one's comfort zone. "Why do I have to take my shoes off in church?" "What is that funny half-bow you do in the aisle of the church?"

While mature adults can usually cope with these differences, understanding that they are largely superficial and do not go to the heart of what it really means to be Christian, little children often have much more trouble with such inconsistencies. "How come the priest at Mummy's church isn't allowed to have kids but the priest at Daddy's church is?" Children need security, the security of a world that is comprehensible to them. This means one that is relatively simple and consistent, at least until they grow old enough to handle the subtleties of our adult human failings that have led to the sad and unbearable splits in the Body of Christ we now endure. This is why we advise couples from different denominations to choose one church and both stick to it with all their hearts, even though this means a large sacrifice for one of them.

In light of this, it is perhaps understandable that some Orthodox churches insist that those who receive their mystery of marriage must both be faithful Orthodox Christians, even if this means that one of the partners must undergo a period of exploration and training in the Orthodox Christian faith before formally converting to it. These conversions are never entered into lightly, nor does the Church ever rush a person to convert, preferring to allow people to make their own decision on their own terms.

To be sure, most such converts would probably not have come to the Orthodox faith had they not fallen in love with their Orthodox partners, but that does not stop a person from seeking to understand and appreciate the Church and finding a strong relationship with God in her. Cradle Christians (those born and raised in a Christian family) do not choose their church initially either, yet they grow to love and appreciate it because it is part of their family structure. In the same way, a non-Orthodox Christian who already espouses values like honesty, truth, compassion, kindness, and so on, will find a great deal to embrace and respect in the Orthodox faith, and with appropriate spiritual guidance and support he can certainly come to a sense of true belonging in the Church.

But How Can I Know?

As we keep repeating, there is no one secret formula, no surefire method for being certain that you are making the right decision. Marriage, like other important things in life such as religious belief, parenthood, or even accepting a new job, is necessarily a step of faith. By all means, we should do everything we can to prepare ourselves for all those things and to use the brains God gave us to avoid making a big mistake. But in the end, marriage is an adventure, a roller coaster ride of ups and downs. If you approach it with the right attitude, it will be one of the most exciting and fulfilling experiences of your life, even the scary bits that nearly make you throw up. But if you approach it with a negative attitude, you will miss all that wonder and excitement, and you will end up feeling sick and disappointed.

We have said all along that such an important decision is one the sincere Christian wishes to surrender to God's will, but what does that mean exactly? Can you expect God to make the decision *for you*? The answer to that question is, "Yes and no."

On the one hand, God has given each of us a unique gift, the gift of free will, a gift that makes us more in His image than anything else in the universe. And He leaves us to exercise that free will without interference, even in choices like whether we wish to marry and whom. It is a part of our responsibility as human agents with free will, and part of our growth as creatures created in the image of God, to exercise that free will with wisdom and care. That is what we contribute to the synergy or cooperation between God and human.

But where shall we find this wisdom? Here is where God steps in, for He is the source of all wisdom and truth. In His love and kindness toward us, He does not leave us alone in our exercise of that gift of free will but constantly offers us His support and protection—at least to those who genuinely seek it.

It is worth spending a little time here to think more deeply about this idea of *synergy*, this cooperation or working together for a common goal. In the anatomy of the body, two muscles are said to work in synergy if they pull a bone in different directions but regulate their force in such a way as to enable the bone to perform complex and finely tuned actions.

When you grasp a cup in your hand so that nothing spills out, you achieve that steadiness by perfectly balancing the pull of the muscles on one side of your arm against the pull of the muscles on the other side. Even though they are actually pulling your arm in opposite directions, they work together so smoothly, in such perfect cooperation, that the overall action seems utterly effortless. Such perfection comes only with years of practice. Just watch a toddler trying to perform the same action and you will understand what we mean.

This synergy is characteristic of a good marriage. Both partners have so fine an understanding of each other and so unified a set of goals in life that they are capable of working together, sometimes even pulling in opposite directions, but in a coordinated way that becomes as beautiful as a subtle intertwining dance. This synergy of marriage is itself an image of the even more beautiful and subtle intertwining synergy between God and your free will.

Sometimes people wish for God to just make the decision for them, much as parents once chose their children's spouses in the era of our great-grandparents. But for God to do so would be for Him to treat you as a child (indeed, in those times girls were often married in their early teens). That is not God's plan for you. He wants you to be free, to be yourself, to grow in wisdom and stature, and to flourish. So instead, without leaving you alone, He allows you to use your God-given mind and heart. To surrender to God's will is not to have Him make the decision for you, but to accept His input into the process of decision-making and to work with Him in an intimate and beautiful synergy.

God can have this input in many different ways. Each

individual couple needs to keep their minds and their ears open to the voice of God. Often, that voice will come through not just one source but many. If a couple are genuinely surrendering their decision to God, willing to follow His wisdom wherever that may lead, and they find that all sources are agreeing on a particular decision over a prolonged period of time, then they can generally be comfortable that they are walking within the will of God. Let us consider some of the ways in which we can experience that wisdom and guidance of God.

Inner Peace

The truth of God has a way of bringing true peace. We feel restless when something is wrong, when something rings false, even if we can't quite put our finger on why. On the other hand, when something is right, when it is fitting and proper, when it works, we feel a sense of serenity. The steps mentioned earlier should help you to assess your feelings toward the relationship going ahead. If you feel a sense of restlessness, perhaps the advice above may even help you to put your finger on where it comes from.

It may happen that all parties feel a deep sense of inner peace about the matter that only grows stronger as time goes on. On the other hand, one or more of the parties may find themselves anxious or restless about the matter. It is quite dangerous to proceed with a marriage if one or more parties do not feel peaceful about it.

Of course, honesty is crucial here (just as it is in our relationship with God). We human beings are masters of self-deception. For example, the phenomenon of *confirmation bias* is well attested in the psychological literature. This is where we tend to notice and heavily weight evidence that agrees with our preconceptions or our desires, while we tend to ignore or give a lighter weighting to evidence that goes against them. The net result is that we come to the conclusions that we want rather than conclusions that are justified.

In this, and in many other ways, it is possible to convince yourself that you feel good about a relationship by covering up or denying the very real anxieties you may be experiencing. This is a sure recipe for disaster in the future. Reality has a way of forcing itself upon us, no matter how strongly we resist it. If there is reason for doubt about a relationship, the engagement period is the time to face it and resolve it one way or another, so do not ignore that niggle.

Harmony with Your Christian Faith

The Bible and our beautiful Orthodox Christian Tradition are the foundations on which we build every aspect of our lives, and marriage is no exception to that rule. It is impossible for God's will to be at odds with God's Word. Always strive to keep in mind the principles and ideals of Christian life as you progress in this relationship. Ask yourself constantly whether you are living up to the ideals of the Gospel: compassion, honesty, respect, truth, and, above all, divine, unselfish love. Is this a relationship based on genuine care for each other, or is it self-seeking? A relationship that is based on greed, selfishness, materialism, lust, lies, or illegality cannot be in harmony with the wisdom and will of God.

The Course of Circumstances

"If it is God's will, it will happen." This is something we often hear, especially in relation to major decisions like marriage. While there is a certain truth to that statement, things may not be that simple. For example, many good and worthy things in life are only achieved through great toil against powerful opposition. Just think of your own personal struggles against sin. A good and pure heart does not just "happen," although it is certainly God's will that each of us have such a heart. So perhaps we should not expect the smoothness of the path to be a clear indication of the rightness of a decision to marry someone. Perhaps the better measure is the one we have just discussed: the *rightness* of the path.

That said, if all parties are truly seeking the will of God for their lives, doing their best to find it and follow it, then they can be confident that God will so arrange their circumstances to make His will happen. The truth of God, like reality, has a way of ultimately asserting itself.

Of course, His will may not be what we expected. It is not uncommon that a couple surrenders the matter to God only to find that everything starts to go horribly wrong. With further prayer, consideration, and advice, they begin to uncover the underlying problems with the relationship. They come to realize that for them to get married would be an unmitigated disaster! Keeping an open mind and seeking truth constantly are essential tools for interpreting the true significance of events and circumstances.

The Agreement of All Concerned

We discussed above the value of seeking the advice of people you trust and respect, people who know you well and love you, such as parents, responsible relatives, old and trusted friends, spiritual guides, and confession fathers. By and large, it is a very positive sign if all these parties are comfortable about the match and raise no major concerns.

If, on the other hand, one or more of them raises major objections, it would be extremely wise not to go ahead until the objection is resolved. If it cannot be resolved, then that too may be the hand of God closing the door. Of course this by itself is not an infallible guide either, since all these people are humans too, with their own motivations and agendas. You will need to weigh any person's opinion against what you know of their general level of reliability, objectivity, and wisdom.

Special Signs

Sometimes, a couple may seek some kind of special sign from God. Perhaps they feel they are not up to the task of making the decision themselves, or perhaps they seek a divine seal on their decision already made. In certain rare circumstances, it happens that God gives a clear sign about a marriage, but this is something of a miracle, and it is as rare as miracles in general are.

Now, in a way, the bread we eat every day is a miracle—that a tiny little seed grows into a tall wheat stalk to provide us with nourishment. It is in some ways just as miraculous as the miracle of the five loaves and two fish. But our daily bread is just one aspect of the miracle of our very existence and the wonder of this natural world.

We live our lives not by depending on Jesus to daily transform five loaves into enough food to fill a supermarket, but by depending on the wisdom and power of His creation in this natural world, in the fields and farms that fill our supermarkets with food daily. Just as we do not depend on special and dramatic miracles in order to live our daily lives, we should not depend on special and dramatic miracles to make decisions like whether and whom to marry. If such a special miracle should happen, it will almost certainly not be because we sought it but because God Himself saw that it was fitting in the circumstances.

One must therefore be extremely careful about interpreting

"signs." Some people are so keen to find a sign that they let their imagination take over and read far more than God ever intended into innocent things. Effects like confirmation bias can come into play here. But God's genuine signs are always unmistakable and in harmony with our faith. We highly recommend that you get guidance and direction from your spiritual guide before accepting anything as a sign.

Some people try to perform an altar lot[4] as a way of leaving their decision up to God. While it is true that there are certain kinds of decisions where this may be appropriate (for example, the final choice of a new Coptic Pope), there are strict limitations on when such a procedure can be properly employed. It is virtually *never* appropriate as a method for choosing one's life partner.

Having carefully built the vessel of your personality and safely navigated the choppy straits of finding and choosing your partner, you are now ready to embark upon the grand ocean voyage of married life together. What is this journey all about? What is its destination? And how can you get there safely? These are the topics of the next chapter.

Reflection Questions on What Engagements Are For

» Why should we feel no regret when an engagement breaks up?
» What kinds of problems might arise if an engagement is too short, or if it goes on too long?

---

4   An altar lot is where two possible choices are written on two pieces of paper, which are then placed on the altar while a liturgy is prayed. At the conclusion of the liturgy, the celebrating priest is asked to blindly choose one of the pieces of paper, which choice is then taken to be from the hand of God.

Reflection Questions on the Five Stages of a Relationship

» What are the five stages of a relationship, and what happens in each of the stages?

» Is it a worrying sign if you are oscillating between stages, going back and forth, over and over?

Reflection Questions on Spirituality During Engagement

» What kinds of spiritual activities do you think you could share with your partner?

» What does a healthy physical relationship during engagement look like?

Reflection Questions on Compatibility

» Is there just *one* right person for each of us in this world? What does it mean, then, to say that your future spouse is the right person for you?

» "Compatible" does not mean "identical." What does this mean?

» Work through the reflection questions under each of the Compatibility subheadings. In what ways are you compatible, and in what ways are you incompatible with your partner? How important are the compatibilities to you both, and how serious are the incompatibilities?

Reflection Questions on Making the Right Decision

» Which of the suggestions provided do you think are the most suitable for your own relationship, and why?

» What are the advantages and pitfalls of considering other people's advice regarding your choice of partner? What principles can you follow to make this advice more effective and less harmful?

Reflection Questions on But How Can I Know?
   » How will you make your decision that your partner is the
      one you should marry? What will it take for you to be able
      to say, "I know this is the right decision"?

CHAPTER THREE

NOT TWO BUT ONE

What Christian Marriage Is

*And He answered and said to them, "Have you
not read that He who made them at the beginning
'made them male and female,' and said, 'For this
reason a man shall leave his father and mother
and be joined to his wife, and the two shall become
one flesh'? So then, they are no longer two but one
flesh. Therefore what God has joined together, let
not man separate."*

(MATTHEW 19:4–6)

*"The two shall be one flesh." For the husband and
wife are one in nature, in consent, in union, in
disposition, and the conduct of life. However, they
are separated in gender and number.*

APOSTOLIC CONSTITUTIONS
(THIRD CENTURY)[5]

---

5   Quoted in *A Dictionary of Early Christian Beliefs,* ed. David W.
Bercot (Peabody: Hendrickson Publishers, 1998), p. 426.

Marriage is honorable among all, and the bed undefiled; but fornicators and adulterers God will judge.

(HEBREWS 13:4)

CHRISTIANS DID NOT INVENT THE EATING OF FOOD, but they still bless their meals, transforming them into an occasion for thanksgiving and communion with God and with one another. In like manner, Christians did not invent marriage, but they bless and transform it in the same way.

Marriage has been a central feature of human life as far back as we can trace it—a means of finding counsel, companionship, security, and support as one progresses through life, and of providing children with the stability and love they need to flourish and grow into healthy and happy adults. We are wired by God's grand design to desire a partner and to join our lives together, to great mutual benefit. This is a human desire and practice that has been blessed and sanctified by the Church through the mystery of marriage.

We need this blessing, because in this fallen world, so beautiful and necessary a thing as marriage can be, and has been, corrupted in many ways that have cheapened, weakened, and even destroyed it. Through the sacramental grace of the Holy Spirit, the Church helps her children reclaim marriage from that corruption and restore it to the glory always intended for it by God. In so doing, we find that the mystery of marriage becomes a major means to our own salvation and to the salvation of the whole world.

In this chapter, we will be looking at what marriage means to the Christian. We will see its spiritual importance and reflect on how that spiritual dimension can infiltrate and saturate our daily lives, transfiguring them into an image of heaven. In this fallen world, inhabited by fallen humans, successful and happy marriages don't just happen by themselves. They require wisdom and understanding, love and self-sacrifice, and most of all, the grace of God.

If you think about it, there are many other ways God could have arranged human life and even reproduction. And yet, of all the possibilities, He chose to bestow upon humanity this alluring, exhilarating, profound, and frustrating thing we call marriage. We can best understand this choice when we consider the place of marriage in our wider spiritual story.

Christian marriage is different because people who are Christian undertake it. That may seem obvious, but it is in fact a very important thing to realize. A Christian may share many of the same reasons that non-Christians have for getting married, such as companionship and providing a stable home for children, but in addition to this, the Christian sees marriage through the lens of the Incarnation and salvation of Christ. Like everything else in our lives, marriage becomes not a goal in itself but a means to the greatest goal of all: our transformation into the image of the God of love.

The goal of our lives on earth, the reason we are born and die and live this life in between, is to experience a little of the existence that is the nature of God and, as freely moral beings, to choose to become beings of life rather than death, of light rather than darkness, of good rather than evil, and of love rather than selfishness. This is what it means not only to be a Christian, but indeed to be a human being in this world, whether you are aware of it or not. But as Christians, we have access to wisdom and guidance from the Bible and the traditions of the early Christians, who received the teachings and practices of Christ and His apostles. In what follows, we will use these resources to help us understand the part marriage plays in our overall lives and in our salvation especially.

Love

"God is love." (1 John 4:8, 16)

Those three little words sum up the essence of the Christian gospel. The God who is love created the world out of His love, giving it that which is His own: existence. In love, He made the world good. In love, He gave each part of the world something of Himself: sheer existence to atoms, growth and re-creation to plants, and souls and actions to animals. And finally, to the pinnacle of this creation—humanity—He gave a self-aware and reasoning mind, a free will, and an eternal spirit.

Humanity is the most accurate (yet still wildly inadequate) image of God there is. Of all that exists in this world, humanity alone is able freely to choose whether to be the image of the God of love or not. In this choice lies the deepest love: a love that is not forced upon the creature by its Creator but can be freely chosen or rejected. This kind of divine love has come to be denoted in Christian circles by the Greek word *agape* (AH-guh-pey).

Marriages begin and continue on the basis of voluntary love. Marriage provides us with a unique opportunity to more fully embody the image of the God of love, giving it a concrete expression here and now. By choosing to love your spouse, by giving yourself to your spouse body, mind, and spirit, by living your life in the selfless service of your spouse, you yourself are changed, transformed, transfigured. You become more and more the true and faithful image of God. "When husband and wife are united in marriage they no longer seem like something earthly, but rather like the image of God Himself."[6] Marriage is one of the ways human beings learn about this true, divine, unselfish, and giving love. It is a kind of laboratory where a person discovers, explores, and acquires the love that will benefit him or her in reaching the Kingdom of heaven.

Sometimes people ask, if God is love, then whom did He love before He created the world, when He alone existed? Did He love Himself? How is that love? Isn't that just selfishness? The answer to these questions lies in the Christian understanding of the Trinity. Before God created the world, when He alone existed, He was still the God who is love, for the Father loves the Son, the Son the Father, and both love and are loved by the Holy Spirit. This circle of love in the Holy Trinity is the deepest nature of God Himself and the basis of the Christian view of the world. All things can only be what they are meant to be when they are faithful reflections of this love.

In a way, what Christ came to achieve in the world was to draw humanity (and the whole world) back into this circle of divine love. "As the Father loved Me, I also have loved you; abide in My love" (John 15:9). We can picture it as three overlapping circles. The top circle is the circle of love that exists between the members of the Holy Trinity, the bottom circle is the circle of human love that exists between us and others, and the middle circle that links the two together, drawing the bottom circle up into the top circle, is the incarnated Christ. As St. Athanasius put it, "He took what is ours, and gave us what is His."

We should therefore not be surprised that Christians have often used human relationships to try to understand the relationship

---

6   St. John Chrysostom, quoted in Fr. George W. Grube, *What the Church Fathers Say About . . .* (Brookline: Light & Life Publishing, 2005), p. 70.

between God and humans. Jesus Himself likened this relationship to that between a Father and His children, and He called His disciples His friends. Marriage is one of the most important of these analogies or "icons" and was used as such by Christ Himself, by His apostles, and by the Church ever since.

An icon in Orthodox Christianity is a sacred image that portrays, mostly without words, a deep, mysterious truth. It is considered to be something like a window looking from our world into heaven, a lens that brings into focus truths that cannot be expressed in mere human language. The mystery of marriage is such an icon, written not with paint on wood, but with human experiences and lives upon the canvas of this world.

In the Bible we find numerous icons of human marriage that reveal to us something about the deep mystery of God's love for us. Some examples are the rich and sensual poetry of mutual love and adoration in the Song of Solomon; the wretched betrayal by the Bride of God in Hosea and Ezekiel 16, and His unconditional and invincible love for her in spite of her unfaithfulness; the joy of St. John the Forerunner at the wedding of Christ and His Bride, humanity (John 3:29); the direct parallel between the marriage of Christ to the Church and of a human groom to his bride (Eph. 5:25–27); and the description of our heavenly state as a "bride adorned for her husband" (Rev. 21:2).

In marrying, you are embarking on a journey that will help to bring you, your partner, and eventually your children to the kind of unity with God for which every human yearns, knowingly or unknowingly. In the laboratory of marriage you will make mistakes and learn from them. You will try things out and discover what works and what doesn't. You will learn the discipline of self-sacrifice that will set you free from the slavery of selfishness. You will make that great discovery that underwrites all creation, the paradox that is the true nature of our existence, that mystery of divine love, so beautifully expressed in what is today known as the Prayer of St. Francis:[7]

Lord, make me an instrument of Your peace;
where there is hatred, let me sow love;
where there is injury, pardon;
where there is doubt, faith;
where there is despair, hope;
where there is darkness, light;
and where there is sadness, joy.

O Divine Master,
grant that I may not so much seek to be consoled as to console;
to be understood, as to understand;
to be loved, as to love;
for it is in giving that we receive,
it is in pardoning that we are pardoned,
and it is in dying that we are born to Eternal Life.
Amen.

All this is very good in theory, you might be thinking, but in practice it is not so easy to live out this kind of agape love. A dozen things can get in the way of our best intentions and end up making us act selfishly. We agree with the sceptic here. Although we

---

7   This beautiful prayer was almost certainly not written by St. Francis of Assisi in the thirteenth century but by an anonymous author near the beginning of the twentieth century. It came to be associated with the saint because it was printed on the back of a small picture of him and distributed widely. It is not hard to see why it came to be identified with St. Francis (or why someone thought to print it on the back of his picture), since his life was undoubtedly a beautiful expression of the sentiments expressed in the prayer.

are to look at some practical ways to make agape love a reality in the next chapter, it is not something we can achieve without God's grace. Left to ourselves, we could never become the kind of being of love we have been describing.

That is why we *need* to be united to the God of love if we wish to truly become beings of love. It is not for nothing that St. John wrote, "We love Him because He first loved us" (1 John 4:19). A human being is only able to love insofar as he or she is loved. A person who is not loved finds it very hard to love others.

So if you are to love your partner, you must first be loved. And of course you are loved, by your parents, family, and friends, and now by your partner. But all of those human loves are imperfect in their love in one way or another—all are time-dependent and fade with distance—all are limited. If you wish to aspire to unconditional love for your partner, you need to be loved unconditionally, and the only perfect source of unlimited, unfading, eternal, and unconditional agape love we have is God Himself.

So not only do we love Him because He first loved us, but because He first loved us we are able to unconditionally love others. Alone, we are utterly incapable of agape love. But when we know and feel God's agape love for us, we become capable of miracles.

The saintly Coptic Fr. Pishoy Kamel used to say that when you give away anything in this world, you end up with less of it for yourself, but the more love you give away, the more of it you have in yourself. This is the nature of love: it multiplies as it passes from one to another. God's love is poured into us and irresistibly overflows from us to others, and from them to others still, and so on in an eternal spreading wave of love. Even when we pass it on to others, we remain just as full and overflowing ourselves. But in order to be a part of this wave, in order to propagate it on to others rather than being the barrier that stops it, we need to give ourselves to it, to surrender and humbly submit.

Humility, Submission, and Surrender

These days, "submission" is a dirty word. So are words like "humility" and "surrender." We are obsessed in modern Western society with preserving the rights of the individual and ensuring that no one is taken advantage of. This is an admirable thing in a fallen world, where selfishness reigns as the chief motivator of our actions, our relationships, and our politics.

But remember that Christianity aims to restore the world to its unfallen state, little by little, and that marriage is one of those fields that Christian spouses stake out and claim for the Kingdom of the God of love. Where love is perfect, there is no need for any talk of "rights" and "protections." Where love reigns, each person *voluntarily* submits to, gives freely to, and seeks the welfare of the other. Talk of rights is replaced by talk of kindness. Laws that forced us to treat one another well are completely replaced by the freedom of joyful, voluntary, unconditional, self-sacrificial love.

It is in this context that the Christian speaks of humility, submission, and surrender in marriage, not in the modern context of selfish power struggles and politics, of necessary rights and protections. Take for example the famous poetic passage about marriage in Ephesians 5:21–33, a passage that is read in most Orthodox Christian marriage ceremonies:

> submitting to one another in the fear of God.
> Wives, submit to your own husbands, as to the Lord. For the husband is head of the wife, as also Christ is head of the church;

and He is the Savior of the body. Therefore, just as the church is subject to Christ, so *let* the wives *be* to their own husbands in everything.

Husbands, love your wives, just as Christ also loved the church and gave Himself for her, that He might sanctify and cleanse her with the washing of water by the word, that He might present her to Himself a glorious church, not having spot or wrinkle or any such thing, but that she should be holy and without blemish. So husbands ought to love their own wives as their own bodies; he who loves his wife loves himself. For no one ever hated his own flesh, but nourishes and cherishes it, just as the Lord *does* the church. For we are members of His body, of His flesh and of His bones. "For this reason a man shall leave his father and mother and be joined to his wife, and the two shall become one flesh." This is a great mystery, but I speak concerning Christ and the church. Nevertheless let each one of you in particular so love his own wife as himself, and let the wife *see* that she respects *her* husband.

Once again we see that marriage is to be understood as the icon of the relationship between the God of love and the humanity He created in love.

Does God ask for His rights or to be protected from humanity? Does humanity ask for its rights or to be protected from God? Of course not, for this is a relationship based on the principle of self-giving. God gives us existence and love and so much more from Himself, from His very nature, and we in turn are truly fulfilled and glorified when our lives and actions, our very beings, become the direct image of that self-giving. In return we offer to Him the little that we have, our hearts and our very lives, as a grateful, willing, and joyful sacrifice. We offer back to Him what is really His, having originated from Him.

That is what the relationship between a husband and wife is supposed to be like, and that is the aim of Christian marriage. But this beautiful reflection of divine love is impossible to attain without true humility, for it is humility that frees us from the chains of the ego and allows us to fly free in unconditional self-giving. As St. Ephraim the Syrian said in the fourth century, "Do you wish to lead a proper life? Then exercise humility. If you refuse to do this, it is impossible to share a love or lead a good life."[8]

But let us take a more practical approach: what does all this mean in real life? Let us say you are married and now have a decision to make—perhaps you must choose which suburb you are going to live in after the wedding. Your spouse wants to live near her parents so they can babysit when the children come along, but you want to live in a suburb that is closer to your work so you don't have to travel too far each day. You discuss it at some length, but neither of you is able to convince the other.

You seem to be at an impasse. How will you get past this? The man might say, "I am the head of the family; my word goes, and you must submit—the Bible says so." But this would be an abuse of the Bible passage above and an act that kills love. How true are the words, "Coercion exercised over the will of another—even in the name of love—kills love itself."[9]

Note that the very first line in the Ephesians passage above directs both the husband *and* the wife to submit to each other. Not just the wife, but the husband also must be submissive. In fact, the husband is called to an even more drastic form of

---

8   Quoted in Grube, op. cit., p. 74.

9   Fr. Alexander Elchaninov, quoted in Fr. John Meyendorff, *Marriage: An Orthodox Perspective* (Crestwood, NY: St. Vladimir's Seminary Press, 1984), p. 97.

submission: he is called to be ready to give his life for his wife, as Christ did for the Church. If his very life is required of him by love, then how much more is required the much smaller sacrifice of living in a suburb that will make his wife feel more comfortable and secure?

When you reach the perfect ideal of love, you will in fact suggest that you live in your wife's suburb of choice despite your own needs, with perfect joy, and your spouse will do the same for you. Such arguments, ones where both argue for the *other's* needs instead of their own, are much more easily and happily resolved than arguments where both are arguing for their own selfish needs. Again, in the words of St. Ephraim, "Arrogance is like a very tall but rotten tree. All its branches are brittle and if someone climbs upon it, he immediately falls from the height he has attained."[10]

Such perfection in love takes a lifetime to achieve, but it must be the goal of every Christian marriage. Marriage is that laboratory, as we said, where we learn love through hard and often painful experience. Through this journey, you are remade, forged anew, purified in the burning fires of divine agape love, and stripped of your pride, ego, stubbornness, and selfishness, until you emerge in your pure and undefiled state, a perfect image of the God of love.

This image is humble, for you will not consider yourself better than your spouse. Instead you will rejoice to be his or her servant, serving the person for whom you have a passion with complete joy and unselfconscious abandon. This image is submissive, not as one who is forced bitterly to bow before a hated enemy, but as a gentle father bows sweetly before a baby to have his nose tweaked, or carries the baby on his back like a beast of

---

10   Quoted in Grube, op. cit., p. 74.

burden. This is the image of surrender, not the surrender of hostile defeat reluctantly accepted because there is no other choice, but the ecstatic surrender into the arms of one who loves you with all his or her being. We have these words from St. John Chrysostom:

> If you think that the wife is the loser because she is told to fear her husband, remember that the principal duty of love is assigned to the husband and you will see that it is her gain. "And what if my wife refuses to obey me?" Never mind! Your obligation is to love her; do your duty![11]

In marriage, it is best not to ask whether your spouse is living up to your expectations. Instead, ask yourself constantly whether you are living up to his or hers. If you both live your lives together this way, there will be nothing but peace, joy, and love between you. But it is crucial to note that *both* partners must adopt this approach. An unbalanced relationship where one partner is unselfish and the other is selfish will also quickly disintegrate. When one or both partners depart from this formula and allow themselves to fall back into selfish and self-seeking ways, when they allow the ego to rear its ugly head, they inevitably fall into discord and disharmony, into hurt feelings and wounded memories, and feel the need for rights and protections once more. To do that is to lose some of the territory of the Kingdom of God to His enemies, and it is we who suffer most for the loss.

---

11   St. John Chrysostom, *On Marriage and Family Life,* trans. Catherine P. Roth and David Anderson (Crestwood, NY: St. Vladimir's Seminary Press, 1986), p. 54.

Unity and Vulnerability

Surrender implies making yourself vulnerable to the one to whom you surrender. This is never an easy thing.

In marriage, you necessarily open yourself up to your partner. There is great joy in doing this, for we live our fallen lives in isolation and loneliness, yearning constantly for intimacy and for the opportunity to share our deepest selves with another. It is perhaps the deepest and most significant yearning that any human being has in his life. But this intimacy comes at a price. In letting another person into your deepest self, you are also making it possible for that person to harm you. When you let a guest into your house, there is always a possibility that the guest will damage your home in some way.

This whole scenario is played out, among other ways, in sexuality. We are wired to desire physical intimacy with another, but this intimacy requires us to make ourselves vulnerable, to allow ourselves to be naked with another person, with all our scars and marks and imperfections. We allow ourselves to be emotionally vulnerable: what if I desire my partner, but she does not desire me, or does not desire me in the same way I desire her? What if he does not find me attractive? What if I am rejected?

Such surrender is incredibly difficult to enact. We have a host of safety mechanisms and warning bells wired into our psyches to protect us from being hurt by others. For example, we are constantly imagining subconsciously how we come across to others, picturing ourselves through their eyes, and making little adjustments to our words and actions in order to give them what we think they want from us. We also have mechanisms for "mirroring" others, and this is one of the ways by which we come to understand the world.

Built-in mechanisms like this mean that we are constantly

reinventing ourselves, changing what we look like to others, rather than enduring the insufferable horror of letting them see our true and unaltered inner selves. And yet, without this surrender, it is impossible to enjoy the unity that results from it. The less I am willing to give my true self to another person, the less I can truly be one with her.

There are a number of reasons why this unity is so important. Firstly, we human beings are social creatures. We not only crave intimacy with others; we don't work properly if we don't find that intimacy. Studies have shown how seriously dysfunctional chimps become when they are deprived of physical contact with their mothers as babies. Even physical contact with furry stuffed toys can allow them to develop more normally. We humans share that need, and marriage provides an opportunity for an intimacy that allows us to be ourselves without fear. This helps us to be healthy, both emotionally and physically. This was depicted in the Bible in the story of Eve's creation from the side of Adam:

> Then the Lord God built the rib He took from Adam into a woman, and brought her to him. So Adam said, "This is now bone of my bones, and flesh of my flesh. She shall be called Woman, because she was taken out of Man. For this reason a man shall leave his father and mother and be joined to his wife; and the two shall become one flesh." (Gen. 2:22–24)

Secondly, this unity with another helps us to become fully ourselves. In surrendering to your spouse, you are not losing your life but finding it. When you share your experiences with your spouse, you see those experiences afresh, not only through your own eyes but through his eyes as well, which brings to those experiences an extra dimension of vividness, meaning, and reality. In making yourself vulnerable to your spouse, you open up areas of your being and personality to her scrutiny. If you can find acceptance there, you yourself grow in confidence and joy.

Being freely and voluntarily loved and accepted is one of the most powerful forces that can act upon us. What is more, Christian salvation involves being transformed and sanctified, and this transformation requires a kind of honesty that necessitates vulnerability. When you are vulnerable to your spouse, there is no longer room for self-deception; you must face the true reflection of yourself that you see in her eyes, with all its beauty and ugliness.

But in Christian marriage, the horror of being exposed is blessed and transformed by your spouse's unconditional agape love, the love that ultimately makes you beautiful in his eyes, and therefore in your own eyes too. And so, when "the two become one flesh," you feel that your spouse is in fact a part of you, and you feel that without her you are incomplete.

Thirdly, "God created Adam and Eve that there might be great love between them, reflecting the mystery of the divine unity."[12] We saw above that the unity between husband and wife is an icon of the unity between God and the human soul. An icon is a small-scale earthly representation of a divine and heavenly truth. In married love, we get a little taste of the divine love we were created to share with our Creator. In being united to your spouse, you get a little taste of what it is to be united to God.

St. John Chrysostom wrote, "Paul says elsewhere, 'The head of Christ is God,' and I say that husband and wife are one body in the same way as Christ and the Father are one."[13] And indeed there are many parallels between the marriage rite and the rite of the Eucharist, which is the marriage rite between us and God. For example, when the priest lifts the *prospherine*, the large cloth

---

12   St. Theophilus of Antioch, quoted in Grube, op. cit., p. 71.
13   St. John Chrysostom, op. cit., p. 52.

that covers the altar, it is like the divine Groom lifting the veil that hangs between Him and His Bride so that they may gaze lovingly upon each other's faces. And of course, at the end of the rite, the two become one flesh, for Christ's Body and Blood mingle with our own in the most intimate way.

We have enough trouble surrendering ourselves and allowing ourselves to be vulnerable to our Creator—is it easier or harder to do so with another weak and faulty human being? On the one hand, it is harder because, while we know that God will not hurt us, we cannot be sure that our spouses will not. On the other hand, it is in many ways easier to deal with your spouse, whom you can see and touch and with whom you can reason. And because this unity and vulnerability are imbued with divine agape love, this reasoning takes place in a safe environment that allows honesty to flourish.

> Two souls united this way have nothing to fear. With harmony, peace and mutual love, husband and wife possess every possible wealth. They can live in peace behind the impregnable wall which protects them, which is love in accordance with God's will. Thanks to love, they are harder than a diamond, harder than iron, they have everything they need as they steer their course toward eternal glory, and enter more and more fully into God's grace.[14]

Metanoia (Repentance and Change)

In Chapter Two we considered the need for people to grow and to change before they start looking for a partner, but we also pointed out that this is a process that continues throughout the whole life of the sincere Christian. The environment of honesty and

---

14   St. John Chrysostom, quoted in Grube, op. cit., p. 73.

vulnerability within a marriage is the ideal place to practice this basic Christian principle of *metanoia*.

This word of Greek origin literally means to change one's mind or way of thinking and is usually translated into English as "repentance." When you are single, you strive to improve yourself for your own sake. But once you are committed and in a married relationship, the motivation becomes even stronger—you are now responsible to work on yourself so that you can make your spouse's life better too.

In some ways, marriage makes this process of metanoia easier, for now you are living day after day with your spouse and are forced to see yourself through her eyes. There is no longer the possibility of hiding from obvious and painful truths about yourself.[15] This is a good thing, for you are blessed with a devoted and loving partner who is willing to support you, love you, and nurse you through the painful and difficult process of change that is metanoia. And of course, you will return the favor by doing the same for him.

Salvation

This ongoing process of purification through metanoia with mutual encouragement and support is but one way that marriage helps us to attain salvation. Marriage works for our salvation not just by helping us to eliminate what is negative from our lives, but also by helping us to build what is positive.

What must we do to be saved? The simplest summary can be

---

15 Having children multiplies this effect many times over. There is nothing so good for the soul as hearing your children pick out your faults ruthlessly one by one as they grow up and learn more about life. But that is a topic for another time.

found in the dialogue between Christ and the lawyer, and the answer to the question, "Which is the most important of all God's laws?" Jesus replies, "'You shall love the LORD your God with all your heart, with all your soul, with all your strength, and with all your mind,' and 'your neighbor as yourself'" (Luke 10:27). As one of the desert Fathers said, "no one is saved alone, but our salvation lies with each other."

Since our salvation chiefly depends on our becoming the image of God, the God of love, it is in living a life of love that we find our salvation. By performing acts of love toward God and toward others, we are gradually transformed into "beings of love," in the image of God who is love. The more we become this kind of being, the more we belong in heaven.

The marriage relationship provides uncounted opportunities to perform these little acts of Christlike kindness, opportunities to practice the kinds of things that make us fit for heaven: long-suffering, compassion, forgiveness, patience, and unconditional love. What is more, as time goes on, you may find yourself performing them with little thought of being thanked or appreciated. You are now acting out of truly unselfish love, out of a pure and undiluted desire to give, seeking nothing in return from the receiver. You are becoming a true image of God.

In this way, marriage commits you to being at least partially responsible for the salvation of your spouse and, eventually, for your children. You are committing to help and support your spouse to live a life that will allow her to be worthy of the Kingdom of heaven.

This includes creating a home where the environment is conducive to such a life, a place that can truly be described in the words of the ancient litany as one of the "houses of prayer, houses of purity, houses of blessing."[16] Those words describe our aspirations for the Church itself, but as we shall see below, in marrying, you and your spouse are creating a new little outcrop of the Church in your own home, and everything that applies in church should also apply in your new home. "Marriage is more than human. It is a 'microbasileia,' a miniature kingdom, which is the little house of the Lord."[17]

The Church is the Body of Christ, and its members are the temples of the Holy Spirit. That applies just as much in your home on Monday as it does in your parish on Sunday. As the Church works to build the Kingdom of heaven right here on this earth, reclaiming the corrupted world little by little, so also each Christian family represents a little more of this fallen world being sanctified by love, purified by self-sacrifice, and so reclaimed for the Kingdom.

Loyalty

As you work together for your own salvation and the salvation of others, you find that this too helps to bind you closer together. In the ancient Greek language of the New Testament there were four different words, each with a different meaning, that may be translated by the single English word "love."[18] We spoke of the most important of these, *agape*, in the first section titled "Love" above. But a marriage, like our relationship with God, is built upon the other three as well. *Storge* is familial affection, the love

---

16 From the Litany of the Congregation, the third of the Three Great Litanies in the Coptic rite.

17 St. Clement of Alexandria, quoted in Grube, op. cit., p. 71.

18 A beautiful account of these types of love and their interrelationships is found in C. S. Lewis's book, *The Four Loves*.

between parents and children and siblings. *Philia* is the love between friends, motivated by common interests. *Eros* is romantic love, the love expressed in physical affection.

These three other kinds of love can be a blessing or a curse in our lives, and especially in a marriage. For example, familial love (storge) practiced selfishly can lead to overbearing or overprotective spouses or parents. Friendship (philia) practiced selfishly can lead to elitism and being uncharitable to others. Physical love (eros) practiced selfishly is mere lust and can lead to emotional, sexual, and physical abuse. All three left to themselves have the potential to do great harm to a marriage and to those who partake of it. But if they are brought under the rule of the fourth kind of love—divine love or agape—they are transfigured and made holy, thus acquiring a great power for good.

Loyalty within marriage is an excellent illustration of this principle of agape transforming the other loves. Loyalty, of course, can be an important manifestation of each of the four loves, but it can be harmful or helpful, depending on whether it is transfigured by agape. To see this, consider both the transfigured and the untransfigured forms of loyalty in marriage. A fierce loyalty to your spouse that is not based on unselfish, unconditional, giving love might express itself in insane jealousy or undue possessiveness. The husband who cannot bear his wife even talking to another man justifies his jealousy by appealing to his care for her and his noble intention to protect her from unscrupulous wolves. This is undoubtedly a kind of loyalty, but it is one that will soon suffocate the relationship.

Similarly, the wife who stands by her husband even when he is wrong, defending and justifying actions that have clearly damaged and wounded others, sees herself as being a loyal wife, even though her fierce, blind loyalty might be enabling the repulsive behavior of her husband and hindering him from repenting of such behavior. But of course these misuses of loyalty should not make us fear loyalty itself. Rather, we need to understand its proper use and role in marriage.

The world outside Christianity has mostly viewed marriage as a contract between two people.[19] As such, it can also be broken if one of the two does not fulfill his obligations, or by mutual consent. But if marriage is meant to be an icon of divine love and the relationship between God and the human being, then it must be much more than a breakable contract between two human parties.

True friends (those who are not in the friendship merely to have their own selfish needs met) do not break their friendship because one party did not fulfill her obligations, for there is more to a friendship than a cold deal or contractual arrangement. In friendship, there is loyalty, and this loyalty takes us from the level of mere rights and privileges up into the level of love that transcends such merely self-preserving arrangements.

Contracts are made to protect your rights. Love does not seek its own protection, as we saw above, but for the sake of the other allows itself to be vulnerable to the beloved, for love would rather be harmed than cause harm. This love begets loyalty in a marriage. I remain loyal to my spouse even if she hurts and wounds me, for that is the nature of love, the love that is able to defeat all other powers in this world.

This loyalty is not limited to the married couple but extends also to the children of the marriage. We love our children no

---

19 At least as far back as Roman law, marriage was viewed as a contract (Meyendorff, op. cit., p. 17). Today in secular Western culture, with the advent of no-fault divorce laws, prenuptial agreements, and the like, the wheel has come full circle, and marriage is once again seen as a mere contract, devoid of spiritual significance.

matter how much they hurt us or disappoint us. In this we are not showing weakness but divine love. This is the love and the loyalty with which Christ loved us—giving Himself freely to us, even when we hated and crucified Him, continuing to strive for our salvation even when others desert us, and even when we desert Him. It is this kind of loyalty sanctified by divine agape love that lies at the heart of the Christian command for couples to make their relationship a lifelong one. Hence the preferability of marrying only once in life:

> Let deacons be the husbands of one wife, ruling *their* children and their own houses well. (1 Tim. 3:12)

> Now to the married I command, *yet* not I but the Lord: A wife is not to depart from *her* husband. But even if she does depart, let her remain unmarried or be reconciled to *her* husband. And a husband is not to divorce *his* wife. (1 Cor. 7:10–11)

This kind of loyalty allows a marriage to become something very special indeed. It provides us with security in difficult times, when we feel the entire world has turned against us. It provides us with comfort in times of loss and loneliness. It provides us with friendship and companionship on which we can depend even when all others fail us. How nice to know that there is someone in the world who will stand by you through all the troubles and tribulations of life and share and magnify your joy in the happy times!

This loyalty is built on truth, for only a true friend loves you enough to tell you when you are wrong. It is this loyalty that preserves the relationship, even through confrontations and disagreements, and turns these experiences into an opportunity for growth as a person rather than a loss. With such loyalty to one another, a married Christian couple hold hands and lead and support each other to the end of their mutual journey to be with God in eternity. This tender strength is beautifully illustrated in the following ancient passage:

> Tell her that you love her more than your own life, because this present life is nothing, and that your only hope is that the two of you pass through this life in such a way that in the world to come, you will be united in perfect love. Say to her, "our time here is brief and fleeting, but if we are pleasing to God, we can exchange this life for the Kingdom to come. Then we will be perfectly one, both with Christ and with each other, and our pleasure will know no bounds. I value your love above all things, and nothing would be so bitter or painful to me as our being at odds with each other. Even if I lose everything, any affliction is tolerable if you will be true to me."[20]

Purity

One expression of married loyalty is exclusive intimate access to your spouse's heart and body. Physical intimacy is holy and blessed within the marriage relationship, and marriage means giving your whole life to one other person—mind, body, and feelings—as we saw earlier. It involves being committed to a lifelong love and trust in one another.

It is only in this context that sexual relations can be practiced to their fullest potential and true meaning. Christianity considers sex outside this kind of relationship to be a degradation of something noble and beautiful. Marriage allows people to express their sexual desires in a holy and blessed manner, furthering their

---

20   St. John Chrysostom, op. cit., p. 61.

growth as creatures in the image of God, rather than in the shallow, selfish, and meaningless way in which sex outside of marriage is often practiced.

Marriage then becomes not only a means of expressing divine love. It is also a way of protecting oneself from selfish and lustful uses of sex that diminish us as human beings and reduce us to the level of animals, which act on instinct alone. It makes perfect sense to say that a married person who is sexually active with his or her spouse is spiritually "pure," for what could be more pure than engaging in acts sanctified by divine love?

Thus the author of Hebrews calls the marriage bed (meaning the practice of sexual love within marriage) "undefiled." It is a response to those who would say that even within marriage, sex is something that is somehow evil or impure but must be reluctantly tolerated. We must remember that Adam and Eve were commanded to "Be fruitful and multiply; fill the earth and subdue it" (Gen. 1:28) *before* the Fall, not after it. While our fallen nature can and often does corrupt our sexuality, it is important to remember that sexuality is itself a part of the good creation of God, not a consequence of the Fall of humanity.

Creation

In the Old Testament, the chief purpose of marriage was seen as procreation, the production of children so that one's line could continue. To that end, sometimes taking multiple wives or even concubines was seen as acceptable, as in the case of Abraham, Sarah, and Hagar. In the Old Testament, people had little conception of an eternal life with God (since Christ had not yet come), so they were focused on earthly goals, chief among which was the continuation of their family line.

But in the New Testament, Christ raises us above such cares for temporary goals in this temporary world and invites us to transcend them and strive for eternal goals. Chief among these is the goal of becoming the image and likeness of the Living God and becoming one with Him. For the Christian, then, procreation must be seen within this context. It becomes just one more means by which we achieve that goal.

In Christian marriage, having children is seen as the privilege of partaking with God in an act of creation. Through the bond of love in marriage, through the unity of love in the body, we human beings become the instruments of the creation of a new life, a new human being, complete with her own unique personality, character, and spirit. As parents we participate in the molding and shaping of that new life, doing our best in unselfish love to help that person we have created in synergy with God to become himself the image of God.

Thus marriage provides a secure and stable environment in which children may grow and flourish. Children need this security in order to develop into successful and emotionally healthy adults. It is now a well-established fact that children of separated or divorced parents have significantly higher levels of emotional and mental problems than children of stable marriages. The sad fact that broken homes are becoming so common, with all the unnecessary suffering this inflicts on children, is a consequence of ignoring the "Manufacturer's instructions"—God's commandments for how human beings can function properly as they were created to do.

Service

The Christian couple participates with God not only in His act of creation but also in many other aspects of His work for the salvation of the world. Remember that it is our goal as Christians to redeem the world, little by little, transfiguring it from its fallen, broken state back into the holy and whole Kingdom of God. As you experience love and grow in love through marriage, love will naturally spread beyond the marriage relationship itself and out into the rest of the world. Within the family unit there is mutual support and encouragement that allows each member to serve God and His children, thus bearing good fruits in the wider community.

There have been and continue to be many blessed couples, or even whole families, who together have served God in ways they could never achieve alone. As you get to know each other's gifts and passions better, you will find that there is great mutual benefit in supporting each other in whatever way you find to serve God and His world. And the world itself will benefit from your service.

This is something that was clearly understood and encouraged from ancient times. For example, St. John Chrysostom advises young couples to make their wedding feasts (or receptions) appropriate to the sanctity and spiritual beauty of the mystery of marriage they are intended to celebrate. Rather than inviting bands and dancers and serving strong drink, he says, why not invite Christ in the form of the poor and the needy?[21]

We must admit to being stunned at the cost of some wedding

---

21 "Don't hire bands or orchestras; such an expense is excessive and unbecoming. Before anything else, invite Christ. Do you know how to invite Him? 'Whatsoever you do to the least of My brothers,' He said, 'you do to Me.' Don't think that it is annoying to invite the poor for Christ's sake" (St. John Chrysostom, op. cit., p. 79.)

receptions these days, as well as their sometimes very unvirtuous tone. Will your wedding reception be one where Christ will feel He is welcome? Will it be an experience that builds people up, or one that corrupts them? The Christian does not cease to be a servant of Christ during the wedding season. The tone you set from the early stages of your relationship has a good chance of defining how you will continue in the future. How inspiring is this description of the married Christian couple from the third century:

> What kind of yoke is that of two [Christian] believers? It is of one hope, one desire, one discipline, and one and the same service. Both are brethren; both are fellow servants. There is no difference of spirit or of the flesh. Where the flesh is one, the spirit is one too. Together they pray; together they prostrate themselves [bow]. They perform their fasts together, mutually sustaining. They are both equally in the church of God; equally at the banquet of God; equally in straits, in persecutions, in refreshments. Neither has to hide from the other; neither shuns the other; neither is troublesome to the other. With complete freedom, the sick are visited and the poor are relieved.[22]

Reflection Questions on Love

» What does agape love mean? How does it differ from other kinds of love, and how is it meant to relate to other kinds of love?

» In what ways is marriage an icon or image of the love between God and humanity?

---

22 Tertullian, quoted in Bercot, op. cit., p. 425.

Reflection Questions on Humility, Submission, and Surrender
- » What is the difference between the modern secular meaning of words like "submission," "surrender," and "humility," and the Christian meaning of those words?
- » What will submission, surrender, and humility look like in your relationship with your partner?
- » Why is it crucial that *both* partners practice agape love, submission, surrender, and humility, not just one?

Reflection Questions on Unity and Vulnerability
- » Where does our yearning to be united with another come from?
- » Why is vulnerability both shockingly frightening and inexpressibly beautiful?
- » How comfortable do you feel now about making yourself vulnerable to your partner? Is this something that will take time to develop?

Reflection Questions on Metanoia (Repentance and Change)
- » What exactly does the Greek word *metanoia* mean?
- » In what ways can marriage help you to attain metanoia?

Reflection Questions on Salvation
- » In what ways can marriage help you to attain salvation together?
- » In what ways is your home like the Church?

Reflection Questions on Loyalty
- » What are some ways loyalty can go bad?
- » What will being loyal to each other mean in your relationship?

» What are some reasons Christianity teaches that we should marry just one person, not more?

Reflection Questions on Purity
» "A married person who is sexually active with his or her spouse is spiritually 'pure.'" What does this mean?
» How will you keep your marriage pure?

Reflection Questions on Creation
» Why is the mystery of marriage an important foundation for the healthy development of children?
» Have you discussed the possibility of having children with your partner? Are you aware of her views on the matter?

Reflection Questions on Service
» Are there ways that you and your partner can serve together and thereby achieve more than either of you could achieve alone?
» What will your wedding reception be like? Will it be in keeping with your Christian values and a blessing for those who attend it?

CHAPTER FOUR

TWO AS ONE

Living the Dream

Then I returned and saw vanity under the sun:
There is one, and there is not a second one,
And he has neither son nor brother.
And there is no end to all his labor,
Neither is his eye satisfied with wealth.
But he never asks,
"For whom do I labor and deprive myself of
    goodness?"
This also is vanity and a painful distraction.
Two are better than one
Because they have a good reward for their labor.
For if they fall, one will lift up his companion.
But woe to him who is alone when he falls,
For there is not a second one to help him up!
If two lie down together, both stay warm,
But how can one stay warm alone?
If one is added strength, two will stand before him,
And a threefold cord is not quickly broken.

(ECCLESIASTES 4:7–12)

My sister, my bride,
How beautiful are your breasts.
How much more beautiful are your breasts than
    wine,
And the fragrance of your garments than all the
    spices.

(SONG OF SONGS 4:10)

IN THE LAST CHAPTER WE EXPLORED THE BEAUTIFUL ideal of Christian marriage. In this chapter, we turn to the practicalities of how to make it happen. Every couple dreams of living a happy and contented life together. They dream of having the kind of relationship in which they will find support, encouragement, and acceptance, being able to share their experiences and emotions openly and honestly. As we have seen above, this is indeed God's plan for marriage. But that doesn't mean it's going to happen automatically. As with anything really precious in life, you have to work hard to make it happen and keep working hard to keep it going.

Having a great married life is magnificent, but it is by no means easy. It requires time, effort, patience, humility, and much more. When you get it right, you realize that it was worth all the effort, for it is one of the most beautiful and fulfilling experiences human beings are able to have. It is indeed a little slice of heaven on earth. Sadly, many people do not get it right, and we live in a society where a married couple is quite likely to end up divorced rather than remaining married until death parts them. Breakups often involve innocent children who suffer greatly through the anguish of the process of divorce. The statistics in the Orthodox community are better, at least anecdotally, but there is still a worrying trend in recent times toward marriages falling apart.

In our experience, we have found that good premarital counseling makes a significant difference to a marriage's chances of success, and that is one of the things that motivated us to write this book. You see, no one is born knowing how to have a successful, fulfilling marriage—it is something we all have to learn, often the hard way. Just as no one expects you to be a first-class racecar driver the first time you ever sit behind the wheel of a car, no one expects you to be an expert at the complex art of the intense, intimate relationship that is marriage on the wedding night.

One of the things that can really help make a marriage prosper is the couple investing some time and effort into understanding how relationships work, what makes them flourish, how they can go wrong, and how to avoid the pitfalls. For this reason, the focus in this chapter is on the practicalities of the marriage relationship.

We believe that if you prepare yourself for marriage adequately (see Chapter Two), make your choice of spouse wisely (Chapter Three), embrace the meaning of Orthodox Christian marriage wholeheartedly (Chapter Four), are willing to work on your marriage relationship constantly (this chapter), and work through difficult issues wisely (Chapter Six), there is every chance that you will indeed have the long and happy marriage everyone dreams of. Below are some insights and suggestions about what makes for such a successful, fulfilling marriage, rather than one that fails to everyone's harm.

Living Together in Christ

We saw above that when a couple marries, they are establishing a new little outpost of the Church, of the Kingdom of God on earth. Just like the church you attend on Sunday, your new home requires conscious effort and loving care if it is to be what you and God want it to be. At the heart of this little church in your home, just as at the heart of the Church, lies the individual's relationship with God.

When a parish is populated by people who are sincere in their faith and practice—true images of God—things always work out well in the end, for divine agape love is more than a match for any trial, tribulation, or temptation. But where such love is lacking, so also will there be a lack of peace and joy. So your first and most important task as a marriage partner (and later as a parent) is to maintain your own personal unity with Christ. You do this not for your own sake alone, but also for the sake of your spouse and your children.

There are many resources on how to maintain this sincere Christian life, so here we will simply list the chief tools that are useful for this purpose and relate them to married life in particular.

The Bible is God revealing Himself to you, so reading the Bible together and discussing its lessons with your partner is a great habit to institute as early as possible in the relationship. Wonderful new understandings and applications of God's Word are to be found when you read it through someone else's eyes and experiences. Accountability comes through sharing together how well or how poorly you have applied the principles of the Bible.

Prayer is you revealing yourself to God. We encourage every newly married couple to institute a time of communal prayer together every day. It need not be elaborate or long. It may be as simple as each saying a brief prayer from the heart, or praying the Lord's Prayer with one voice, side by side. This practice brings many benefits. For example, it is hard to remain angry with each other when you must both stand before the Great Judge, who taught us that if we wish our own sins to be forgiven, we must first forgive the sins of others (Matt. 6:14).

We have known couples who insisted every night on not only praying together, but also on offering each other a prostration and asking for forgiveness in case they had in any way offended each other throughout that day. We all sin. We all make mistakes. It is far better to have an atmosphere of forgiveness in a relationship than an atmosphere of constantly holding grudges. Remember that even if you are in the right today, one day you yourself will need to be forgiven.

When children come along, there is no better way to teach them the life of prayer than by living it with them. Children learn far more from what they see you do, and from what they do themselves, than from what they are told.

Sharing in the mysteries together is also an important reflection of our shared commitment to Christ and to being united with Him. In order to partake of the Eucharist, we must be reconciled with each other. Regular communion together has a way of constantly resetting the relationship dynamics to "peace" before things can spiral out of control. Partaking of Holy Communion takes on an added dimension of love and unity when a family does it together.

Similar things could be said about other spiritual practices, such as celebrating feasts and observing fasts, performing prostrations, singing hymns, reading and discussing spiritual books, following the church calendar of commemorations, pilgrimages, service to others, and so on. All these spiritual practices help us to understand and know each other better and to feel closer to each other. They bring people together around Christ, bringing them closer to each other as they each individually move closer to the center, which is Christ.

The benefits of a vibrant spiritual life accrue not only to your relationship together but also of course to your own flourishing as a Christian and as a person. The fruits of the Spirit—love, joy, peace, patience, kindness, goodness, faithfulness, gentleness, and self-control (Gal. 5:22–23)—are the results of unity with God and the ingredients for Christian living both within and outside the home. The stronger you are in your own spiritual journey, the better you will be able to cope with the ups and downs of married life, and the more likely you are to become truly Christlike within the relationship.

For example, what will you do when your partner disappoints you in some way, as is bound to happen? As we saw above, we are only capable of unconditional agape love because we know and feel that God loves us unconditionally. If your foundation in life is God, then you will be able to stand firm upon that foundation and weather the storm of disappointment. You will find refuge and consolation in God's unfailing love for you and, ultimately, forgive and forget, going on with a life of love that is perhaps deeper than it was before. If, on the other hand, your foundation in God is weak, then you will find that you have nothing to fall back on, nowhere to find strength or a reason to persevere.

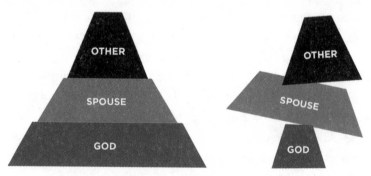

If a person's relationship with God is strong, it can easily support other important relationships, including that with a spouse (left pyramid). When the relationship with God weakens, other relationships may become unstable too (right pyramid).

Wise Counsel

While our experience of the unfailing love of God for us is the bedrock of our relationships, there are times when we feel the need for more direct and immediate guidance than we can generally find in God. So often in a relationship we find ourselves thinking, "I wish I had handled that better. I wish I had been wiser about it. I wish I had someone to teach me what to do and how to do it."

We strive to learn wisdom all our lives, for wisdom makes life run far more smoothly. Wisdom is a gift from God: "The wisdom that is from above is first pure, then peaceable, gentle, willing to yield, full of mercy and good fruits, without partiality and without hypocrisy" (James 3:17). Love is intimately and inextricably entwined with truth, and wisdom is about seeking, finding, and implementing truth. A relationship has to be built on truth to work, like a mathematical argument or a profound novel.

But finding wisdom is no easy thing. Unfortunately, we are not born wise—wisdom is something we have to acquire as we go through life, and it often comes at a significant cost. The happiest and wisest couples are those who see mistakes not as bad things that hurt their feelings but as good things from which they can learn valuable lessons.

One of the ways we can speed up the acquisition of wisdom is to draw upon the wisdom of others. The Book of Proverbs in the Bible often states that seeking advice from a variety of people is a good thing. For example, "Those for whom there is no leadership fall like leaves, / But there is salvation in much counsel" (Prov. 11:12). There is no doubt that, if we see ourselves as lifelong pupils constantly striving to improve our relationships, we can benefit greatly from the experience and advice of others.

But seeking wisdom itself needs to be done with wisdom. Not all advice is equally helpful, and not all advisors are trustworthy all the time. In the worst-case scenario, you might be drawn into the orbit of someone who delights in hearing the private matters of others and then spreading the gossip to all and sundry. Some people push their way into your relationship, seeing themselves as your savior. Some people give very bad advice, but with every indication of utter confidence that it is worth its weight in gold. Then there are advisors for whom some particular approach worked beautifully once in their own lives, and therefore they go about advising everybody else to adopt that particular approach to solve every problem. And some people may have their own agenda, so that their advice will be chiefly aimed at benefitting them, not your relationship.

You can see that seeking advice and wisdom can be fraught with danger. Not all advisors are equal, and even with any given advisor, not all the advice given is equal. Choose your advisors carefully. Check out their qualifications. Professional qualifications mean that a person has undergone rigorous training and is informed by the knowledge base of the profession, which is often a very good thing. In most professions today there are also standards of ongoing professional development that ensure that the practitioner is up to date with the latest research.

But even professional training cannot change a person's basic personality, and some highly trained professionals can be quite narrow in their understanding of human beings or prone to give the wrong advice. It can be helpful to find others who have consulted a particular professional and ask them about their experience before going yourself.

Similar caution is prudent when consulting a spiritual guide, a clergyman or experienced minister within the Church. A clerical uniform does not have magical powers to make the wearer all-knowing or all-wise.

Some in the Church want to transfer responsibility for their personal lives onto a spiritual guide. They find security and relief from anxiety by giving up their own responsibility for rational discernment, subcontracting it out to the spiritual guide (or to the professional), perhaps even depending on him to make all their decisions for them. This can never end well. If you do this, you will never be able to grow and mature as a person or as a Christian. God Himself does not intervene so intrusively into our lives, but rather He leaves us to learn—often the hard way—how to stand on our own two feet. Why then should we think a mere human being can do more than God?

Beware of professionals or spiritual guides who want to make your decisions for you. A good person to go to for counsel is one who takes the role of a coach: supporting, encouraging, guiding, advising, providing experience and wisdom, but leaving you to do all the really hard work and to run the race yourself. If she wants to jump in and run the race for you, you may need to either politely stop this from happening or consider going to someone else.

It is time to turn now from the support network you have in your marriage relationship to the nature of the relationship with your partner itself.

The Importance of Intentions

At the heart of a relationship lie intentions. One of the chief reasons marriages fail is that both members of a couple come to think that the other person does not have their best interests at heart. *Conception of intention* is about what each person believes are the reasons his partner behaves a certain way.

For example, let's say that today you have an important

appointment at three PM, and you have asked your partner to be home by two PM to ensure that you have enough time to get there. Your partner is running late. You may start to think to yourself, "He doesn't care about this appointment, or me for that matter! If he cared for me as much as he cares for his work or other commitments, then he would get here on time. He probably completely forgot!" Imagine how you would then deal with your partner when he walks in the door at 2:10 PM. Most likely, you would radiate anger and disappointment, and of course his response is likely to be a defensive one.

On the other hand, what would happen if you were to think to yourself, "It must have been really hard for her to get out of work so early to come—she normally gets here at seven, so to get here at two would have taken a lot of effort"? How would you greet her as she entered at 2:10 PM in that situation? Probably very differently, and her response would also be different. This is a simple example of something that happens quite often in all relationships over time—people make assumptions about the other person's intentions toward them.

Unfortunately, our assumptions become self-fulfilling prophecies. We start to find evidence that our beliefs are true. We stop asking what the other person means when he says something unexpected and instead interpret his words and behavior according to our own (often mistaken) assumptions about his intentions. When this occurs over a prolonged period of time in a marriage, it can start to erode the relationship and leave each partner believing that the other does not love or care about him or her. Their conceptions of their partner's intentions deteriorate until they become exclusively negative, no matter what the other person says or does.

A marriage is a spiritual union as much as it is a physical, emotional, and social one. If Satan is able to form cracks in that union through corrupting our thinking about each other's intentions, he can then succeed in breaking that relationship. To avoid this, it is imperative to ask your partner in a loving way what caused her to speak or behave in a certain way and be willing to accept that she may have meant something completely different from what you assumed.

Sometimes we misunderstand each other's intentions because we do not understand each other's nature or character. An excellent illustration of this principle is found in the famous and highly recommended book, *The Five Love Languages* by Gary Chapman (see bibliography). In this book the author describes five main ways that people express and feel love: physical touch, words of affirmation, quality time, giving gifts, and acts of service. Each of us tends to prefer one or more of these love languages over the others. When people express their feelings in this language we appreciate it most, and when we come to express love for others we naturally gravitate toward using our preferred love language.

But what happens when you and your partner have different love languages? You then have an opportunity for a disastrous breakdown in interpersonal communication, where words and actions offered with the best of intentions are misunderstood and misconstrued as being the exact opposite.

Take the example of a husband who is moved by love to do something really special for his wife. He goes to a confectioner on his way home from work and spends a long time choosing just the right box of chocolates and writing an eloquent card to attach to them. Beaming, he comes home and surprises his wife with this gift into which he has put so much of himself.

Imagine his surprise when he finds his wife doesn't care about the chocolates. She tosses them aside and starts quizzing him on why he's so late getting home! If he'd received such a lovely box of chocolates and thoughtful card, he would have felt absolutely fabulous. But she's been worried sick about him, and her beautiful, painstakingly prepared dinner has grown cold. What's worse, she's had a terrible day and has been waiting and waiting for him to get home so she could tell him about it and have a good cry on his shoulder. But the longer she had to wait, the more disappointed she got, and the angrier she became with her husband.

It would seem clear that this couple love each other deeply. How is it then that they are now having a major argument? The problem is that they have misread each other and used the wrong love language. The husband's love language is the giving of gifts, so in his mind, he has been extremely thoughtful and loving to his wife. But his wife's love languages seem to be quality time, which he took away from her by tarrying at the shops for so long considering his gift, and acts of service, which he frustrated by staying away so long that the dinner went cold. There are wonderful intentions on both sides but a total lack of understanding of what each needs from the other. The result is a disastrous evening and badly hurt feelings on both sides.

We encourage all couples, in order to avoid situations like this, to take the time to understand the love languages that work best for each of them and to strive to adapt their expressions of love to each other's natures. Ask each other which love language you prefer. Observe each other as you react to the words and actions of others, and discuss these reactions together in order to build a better picture of each other.

Nor is this principle limited to expressions of love. The more you can understand when your partner is happy, when he is bemused, when he is hiding a seething anger, and so on, the better you will be able to see his true intentions, rather than wrongly reading negative intentions into his words and actions. Thus you will be better able to react to her appropriately and effectively. The more this happens, the closer you will feel to your partner.

How to Be United

This closeness that arises from learning to read your partner's true intentions is one expression of that principle of unity that makes marriage so beautiful and so fulfilling. Remember the words of Christ about marriage: "They are no longer two but one flesh" (Matt. 19:6). The more a couple are united in their thoughts, actions, and feelings, the less do they feel that sense of isolation and loneliness that afflicts us in our fallen state of separation from God.

Unity grows out of compassionate love: "Finally, all *of you be* of one mind, having compassion for one another" (1 Pet. 3:8). This love is what allows me to put my selfish needs aside, meet the other halfway, and thus find true unity. It allows me to stop seeking my own and to seek that of my partner, for in doing so I am in fact seeking my own: she *is* me. Enjoy this tender description from the fifth century:

> Because she [the wife] might say, "I haven't spent anything of yours yet; I am still wearing my own clothes bought with the inheritance given to me by my parents." What are you saying, woman? Still wearing your own! And what can be more terrible than this sort of language? Why, you no longer have a body of your own [since it was given to a union through marriage] and you have money of your own? After marriage, you are no longer two, but have become one flesh, and are your possessions

still two, and not of the oneness? This love of money! You have become one person, one living creature, and you can still say "my own"? That cursed and abominable phrase was brought in by the devil. Things that are far nearer and dearer to us than these [material considerations] God has made common to both; are these, then, not also common now? We cannot say "my own light. My own sun, my own water": all our greater blessings are common, and should money not be common? Let the riches be lost ten thousand times over! Or rather, let not the riches be lost, but the frame of mind that doesn't know how to make use of money, and holds it in higher esteem than other things.[23]

Some find it easy to surrender their material possessions to the united relationship but difficult to surrender the importance of their external relationships. Maintaining the unity of the marriage relationship necessarily means not allowing anyone else from outside to interfere, divide, and conquer. Not that people will do this on purpose. Most often it is well-meaning relatives or friends (in-laws are most notorious for this) who cause problems, quite unintentionally.

For instance, suppose you have had a disagreement with your partner, and you spill out your feelings to your mother. Of course, your mother takes your side and comes to share your sense of anger and indignation. But now you are winding each other up, pushing each other to see more and more wrong in your partner, and coming up with ways of teaching him a lesson he clearly deserves (haven't you *both* judged this to be so?). Thus primed, you return home, and somehow the discussion with your partner deteriorates into negativity and defensiveness.

Is it any wonder? Unity is preserved by resolving issues within

---

23   St. John Chrysostom, quoted in Meyendorff, op. cit., p. 88.

the relationship and carefully seeking outside help only when you have truly exhausted all your own resources (or in those rare cases where it is essential, such as abuse or violence, as discussed below). And when you do need that outside help, remember that it is often much safer to seek the help of a trusted spiritual mentor or a professional than to seek the help of relatives or friends, who are more likely to take sides and make things worse.

One of the most dangerous things in a marriage is for a couple to end up feeling as if they are opposed to each other, rather than being on the same team working for the same goals. This is something you must constantly remind yourselves of, especially in times of disagreement: "Hey, we are on the same side." Beware also of embarrassing your partner by strongly disagreeing with her in front of others. This can be one of the most hurtful and divisive things you can do, and few things will drive her away from you more effectively.

Just as important as guarding against division is the active promotion of unity. Make time to do things you both enjoy together, even if work and home put pressure on you. Go out to dinner together, go for long walks by the beach in the moonlight, or renovate the backyard on weekends. Turn off the television and the smart phone when you have dinner, and actually talk to each other. Find out about each other's days and your dreams for the future. Discuss sports or politics or religion. Take an interest in topics your partner finds interesting, and genuinely try to gain a new comprehension of the topics through him. In both positive and negative situations, the ability to put yourself in your partner's place and see the world through his eyes is extremely valuable.

When you allow yourself to walk in the other person's shoes— imagine what it is like to live her life, do her job, and so on—you suddenly see her behavior in a new light. Being empathetic with your wife or husband is about temporarily stepping out of your world and stepping into your partner's. As you express empathy with your partner, you are conveying understanding and allowing him to feel safe and secure in the relationship. Responding empathetically means that you have listened to what your partner is saying, given her your undivided attention, and not provided solutions but reflected her emotions. Such a response is powerful because it reassures the speaker that he is being heard and validated. Being calmer and more secure, he is then better able to hear the other person. Empathy is the calming of any storm. Surprisingly often, all it takes is for one person to express empathy in any argument for it to end.

Personalities in Marriage

One of the wonderful results of learning to empathize is that you find yourself exposed to a whole new world of experiencing *others*. It is said that beauty captures your attention, but personality captures your heart. We are all uniquely and wonderfully made; there are no two people who are exactly the same. Marriage is the best opportunity you will have in your life to enter into the life and personality of another human being and thus have your world significantly expanded.

If your partner were identical to you, this expansion would be limited indeed. While the similarities between you may tie you together, it is the differences that expand your horizons. But taken negatively, the differences that attract you to each other can come to drive you apart, if those differences are scorned rather than celebrated. Learning to appreciate and benefit from your differences will play a big part in the success of your relationship.

There are libraries of books written about personality types and temperaments.[24] We will offer only a brief description of how a couple can use the similarities and differences of their personalities as assets to their relationship, rather than viewing them as obstacles in their path to happiness.

There has been much debate over whether a person is born with a certain personality type or acquires one as a result of his environment: the classical distinction between "nature" (genetics) and "nurture" (experiences). Most psychologists now agree that our personalities are formed by both influences—we are born with a personality type that is then influenced by our environment. Both members of a couple therefore need to talk openly and honestly about their families and their upbringing and be able to share their true selves with their partner.

Most people gravitate toward and end up marrying someone from an opposing personality type. This is usually healthy, because differing personality combinations often balance each other out and ensure that each person's weaknesses are complemented by the other's strengths. This is a little like the way mixed breeds of dogs tend to be healthier than pure breeds.

There are also those who marry people of a similar personality type. When people with similar personalities marry each other, the strengths are doubled, but usually so are the weaknesses of each personality. Honesty about joint weaknesses and strengths is key to the success of same-personality relationships. As a couple it is also important to seek positive outside influence from people with different personality types from each of yours.

Real life is rarely simple. It is extremely unusual for a person to be purely one personality type. Most people are a combination of

---

24   If you are interested in learning more about personality types and their applications, see Florence Littauer, *Personality Plus for Couples* (Ada, MI: Baker Publishing Group, 2001); Keirsey and Bates, op. cit.

two personalities. Sometimes they are balanced evenly, but usually one is predominant. As people grow and mature and have a richer experience of life, they may adopt piecemeal characteristics from other personality types that they find useful or appealing, or as a response to certain situations. For example, a peaceful person may have to learn to be assertive in a work setting, while a popular outgoing person may feel the need to be serious and inwardly focused in times of stress. Therefore, when studying your own or your partner's personality, it is important to remember that no one fits completely into one type.

A variety of ways of classifying personality types have been developed over the years, each with its own strengths and weaknesses. Here we will present a simplified classification that we have found to be both accurate and useful. The Myers-Briggs Type Indicator has sixteen personality types, but Littauer distills these into just four.[25]

> » **Popular:** These are fun-loving, outgoing personalities. They love being the center of attention and thrive on entertaining others. They can (and usually will) talk about anything. They are optimistic, have a great sense of humor, and are fantastic storytellers. Popular personality types often also have some weaknesses, such as being disorganized, lack of attention to detail, exaggeration, appearing not to be serious about anything, and trusting others to do the work for them. Popular personalities are typically attracted to those who will listen to them, laugh at their jokes, praise them, and approve of them (such as precise or peaceful personalities).

---

25 Littauer, op. cit.

» **Powerful:** Powerful personalities are often described as natural-born leaders. They have the ability to take charge of anything instantly and make quick, correct judgments. They can accomplish more in a short time frame. They are confident and restless. They can, however, come across as domineering, insensitive, and impatient and can be unwilling to delegate tasks or give credit to others. Powerful people are naturally attracted to people who are supportive and submissive and who will let them take credit (such as peaceful personalities).

» **Precise:** Precise personalities are highly organized, goal-oriented, and have high standards and ideals. They are also deeply analytical. Their strengths and skills include their sense of detail, love of analysis, follow-through, compassion for those who are hurting, sensitivity, and being meticulous and often well-groomed. However, they, like every other personality type, have weaknesses, such as becoming easily depressed, spending more time preparing than actually doing, becoming too focused on detail, remembering negative things, and being suspicious of others. Precise personalities are often attracted to people who are serious, intellectual, and deep.

» **Peaceful:** Peaceful people have balanced, pleasing personalities. They are usually calm, are great mediators, don't make impulsive decisions, and can be determined to succeed if they are engaged in something they are passionate about. People with a peaceful personality can lack enthusiasm and energy and may be indecisive at times. Peaceful personalities are often attracted to personalities who are comfortable with making decisions and who will recognize their strengths and not ignore them.

Unless a couple embraces the uniqueness in each other's personalities, strengths and weaknesses can get confused with time. What was once an attractive feature of the opposite personality becomes an irritation, and attempts begin to get the other person to be "more like me." For example, the popular personality's once-entertaining storytelling comes to be seen as exaggeration and attention-seeking; the precise personality's money management skills are confused with stinginess; or the peaceful personality's easy-going charm is seen as laziness. Down this road there is only disappointment and resentment, which are totally unnecessary.

The Power of Words

We need to be taught how
to understand one another.

You may think the above statement is ridiculous: "I don't need anyone to teach me how to understand my fiancé(e)!" But the truth is that human beings are complicated creatures, and when two people marry, they often bring very different communication techniques to the relationship. As we keep repeating, the key to success here is to turn differences into positives rather than negatives.

But this is not going to happen by itself. The truth is that most people sooner or later find themselves feeling quite bewildered by something in their partner's behavior or reactions. Unless we make the effort to learn how to understand each other, this bewilderment will become misunderstanding, misunderstanding will become pain, and pain will become anger, disappointment, and resentment. That is how relationships can fall apart.

However good you think your communication skills to be, when you enter into that crucible of marriage, you will discover your shortcomings. Marriage has a way of destroying our over-confidence, which may be a good thing, since this leads us to truth and humility. We are going to need a hefty dose of truth and humility, not to mention love, if we are to take the art of communication seriously.

Above we considered some of the non-verbal ways that we communicate with each other, such as love languages and appreciating each other's personality type. Here, we are going to consider some of the more important and common aspects of how verbal communication works in a relationship and how it can go wrong. But communication skills, like Christlike love, are something that we never finish learning, honing, and improving. As always, prevention is better than cure, but of course, no one can prepare for every possible problem that might arise. Constant vigilance is the only way to be sure you can nip communication problems in the bud before they do serious damage to a relationship.

There is a huge body of literature available today on how to communicate effectively in marriage, and we encourage you to find at least some of the books recommended in the bibliography at the end of this book and work through them together. Taking the time and trouble to properly understand what your partner is communicating to you is an expression of the sincerity of your love for him and of her value in your life. So commit yourself to a lifetime of being a pupil of good communication. There are grave consequences: "Life and death are in the hand of a tongue, / And those who rule over it will eat the fruits thereof" (Prov. 18:21).

Although we communicate in many more ways than just words, it is ultimately *what we say* that our partner hears. Every aspect of communication is important and needs to be considered, but it is words that will make up the greater part of your communication with your partner. Words have the power to heal or wound, to encourage or dishearten, to speak truth or deceive, to praise or criticize. The quality of the life you live depends very much on your words. The success or failure of your relationship is in large part dependent upon the words that you speak. If you speak deep peace and blessings, then you will reap the reward of the inward satisfaction that comes from a harmonious relationship.

A study conducted by Notarius and Markman of Denver University found a fascinating difference between the verbal patterns of couples that stayed together compared to those who did not.[26] With couples that stayed together, only five out of every one hundred comments they made were putdowns. By comparison, with couples that separated, *fifty* out of every hundred comments were putdowns. In study after study, it has been found that the single most reliable predictor of success or failure in a relationship is the kind of words the couple speak to each other. "Hostile put-downs act as cancerous cells that, if unchecked, erode the relationship over time. In the end, relentless unremitting negativity takes control and the couple can't get a week without major blowups."[27]

Just as negative words destroy a relationship, so positive words build it up: "For 'He who would love life / And see good days, / Let him refrain his tongue from evil, / And his lips from speaking deceit" (1 Pet. 3:10). When you approach another person with words of love and praise, that person is more likely to listen to you and receive what you say. Telling your partner that you believe in him and encouraging him enhances both your relationship

---

26 Clifford Notarius and Howard Markman, *We Can Work It Out: How to Solve Conflicts, Save Your Marriage, and Strengthen Your Love for Each Other* (New York: Perigee Books, 1993).

27 *U.S. News and World Report*, February 21, 1994, p. 67.

and your partner's individual success. It is therefore important to remember that sincere compliments and praise energize and encourage action. As you raise the standard of the words you speak, the quality of your relationship will improve, and the quality of your life will increase.

Communication is a two-way street. People are often very good at talking but not nearly so good at listening—yet listening is far more important. Through listening, we learn to understand how the other person is thinking and feeling. We can then respond in a way that is appropriate and more likely to be fruitful. If we don't listen well, misunderstandings happen, and small problems can quickly develop into major disasters.

This is a reflection of that basic Christian principle of agape love. Relationships work when each partner sacrifices his ego and turns instead to look outward, at the other partner. A person who doesn't listen is a person for whom others are less important than herself. Agape love, on the other hand, rejoices and delights in looking outward, in listening with care to the other. It wants to discover the truth of what the other actually wants to say rather than being satisfied with what it thinks the other is saying. When two people have this approach to communication, it is not only much harder for things to go wrong between them, but the quality of their life together is so much richer.

The Way We Speak and Act

While the content of our words is critically important, as we said above, we must not neglect the *way* we say things. Sometimes you can hurt your partner not so much by *what* you say as by *how* you say it.

How we express anger is perhaps the most obvious illustration of this principle. Anger is an emotion that has a broad range of intensity—from minor annoyance to sheer rage. Each of those levels of anger can be expressed in a bewildering variety of ways, often depending on how people saw anger modeled in front of them when they were children. There are constructive, healthy expressions of anger that are essential to the growth and development of any relationship, as well as counterproductive and damaging expressions, such as the shouting match, the sullen silence, the passive-aggressive comment, and distant emotional withdrawal, to mention just a few.

It is important to note that anger is often a mask for other, more painful emotions. Beneath anger there may lie fear, hurt, humiliation, rejection, or a sense of abandonment. Since anger is accompanied by energy, it is easier to express anger than it is to express the root cause that lies behind it. For a person to express fear, hurt, or a sense of rejection or abandonment in a relationship requires him to be vulnerable and exposed to another human being, to risk being hurt further. We find it easier to express anger than to express emotions that leave us vulnerable.

A wife who is angry with her husband because he does not arrive at their appointments on time may be feeling hurt or abandoned. She takes his lateness to mean that he does not value her or that she is not as important to him as his other commitments, which he seems to have no problem in attending punctually. If this couple deals only with her anger, he will naturally respond with self-defense, and her feelings of abandonment and hurt may never be addressed or resolved. Worse still, those negative feelings will probably grow and gain momentum, only adding energy to that anger and escalating it to a higher intensity.

We are hard wired to react to anger in others in certain ways. When you express your anger toward someone, their natural response is to reflect that anger back at you. Hearing an angry voice and seeing an angry face release the hormone adrenaline into the bloodstream, which raises the blood pressure and speeds up the heart rate. This physical reaction stimulates an emotional reaction, and the emotional reaction brings with it angry thoughts in the mind. However, this reaction to anger is not one that will help you as a couple to address the deeper issues that cause the anger.

On the other hand, if anger is actually met with empathy and calmness, rather than defense and retaliation, then a person will feel safe enough to be vulnerable and express her actual fears. As a couple, it is vital that you expect and prepare for anger within your relationship and that your relationship is a safe place to be open and honest about fears and insecurities. It is worth remembering this when you are angry with one another so you can use this knowledge to temper the way you speak to each other.

Does this mean you can reach a stage when you are never angry at all? New couples often fear anger. They consider it to be a sign that something has gone wrong with the relationship, perhaps even a sign that the relationship is deteriorating. But like most things in life, anger itself is morally neutral—it is how we express it and react to it that makes it a good or a bad thing. If we habitually express it in a damaging way, if we allow it to dominate us, it becomes a source of suffering and harm.

No one really *likes* being angry, and certainly not all the time. But St. Paul counsels us, "Therefore, putting away lying, 'Let each one of *you* speak truth with his neighbor,' for we are members of one another. 'Be angry, and do not sin': do not let the sun go down on your wrath, nor give place to the devil" (Eph. 4:25–27). Why is St. Paul giving his stamp of approval to our anger? We must remember that being a true Christian means being *real*, being *authentic*. Notice that St. Paul first counsels us to be true before giving his advice about anger. Anger is a natural part of our behavior and our lives, and it is a normal part of all relationships to some degree. To merely cover up anger, or to pretend that one is above getting angry, is to deny a very real aspect of our nature, one that God Himself created in us.

If a successful relationship needs to be based on authenticity, we must find the right way to handle anger so that it becomes a blessing and not a curse in our lives and relationships. The successful relationship is not necessarily one that eliminates anger altogether but one that has healthy and honest expressions of anger. As with all our instincts and emotions, we must tame anger rather than let it run wild and tear us to pieces.

Anger is a powerful motivator to change, and it needs to be expressed appropriately to drive change for the better. The correct response to poverty and injustice in the world is anger, and this anger motivates us to raise money for the poor and to speak out on behalf of the oppressed. Anger motivates us to strive to heal the evil that is in the world. When we harness anger to play a similar role in the much smaller arena of our personal relationships, it can be just as effective.

This harnessing can take a variety of forms. First, anger can be the catalyst that brings hidden issues to the surface where they can be dealt with. Healthy expressions of anger within a relationship help each person express their concerns or frustrations in a safe environment. This is much healthier long-term than sublimating or denying those issues and the anger to which they give rise. Such denial will usually lead to a build-up of pressure and resentment over time that explodes catastrophically when it can no longer be ignored. Anger can be used to initiate a process of cooperatively and compassionately bringing the deeper issues to the surface so they can be dealt with effectively.

There is then a wisdom to be applied in how we deal with our anger. Anger that rightly reflects a deeper issue in the relationship is an opportunity for the growth of the relationship and can ultimately lead to it becoming stronger. We sometimes think it kinder not to make a fuss, to just sit on our feelings and pretend that everything is fine. But as author John Gray notes, when negative feelings are suppressed, positive feelings are suppressed as well, and love dies. Resolution of issues is much healthier for the relationship than mere suppression.

The second way anger can be harnessed for the good of the relationship is by using it as an opportunity to grow closer together. Sharing an emotional experience of any kind tends to bind people together emotionally, so long as there is a positive outcome by the end. The happy outcome is going to require you both always to base your interaction on a rock-solid commitment to each other. You are partners working cooperatively—even through anger—for a common goal: a happy and fruitful life together.

If teammates in a football team or musicians in an orchestra allow anger to run riot among them, their project suffers, and they are far more likely to lose the match or make a mess of the performance. Who wins then? On the other hand, if they see each other's anger as a sign of their commitment to the success of the team, the anger will most likely motivate them to grow as a team and produce better results together.

The process of harnessing anger to achieve these beneficial goals is a skill that we learn through experience and reflection. It works best where there is a mutually agreed-upon limit to the acceptable duration of the expression of anger, as St. Paul advised above ("do not let the sun go down on your wrath"). This gives you both a way of moving from the expression of anger to the honest exploration of the issues that underlie it and their resolution. All of this is in fact just a reflection of an important aspect of divine agape love: kindness.

There is a vast difference between the emotion of *anger* on the one hand and *aggression* on the other. Whereas anger (expressed appropriately) is an important, honest, natural, and healthy emotion, aggression is a destructive form of expression that involves hurting another person emotionally, psychologically, and/or physically. As odd as this may sound, anger can be expressed with kindness. Aggression generally can't. Purely selfish and unbridled aggression that makes me feel better in the short term, but wounds my partner horribly, is a sin that needs to be repented of by digging out its roots of self-centeredness and replacing them with compassion.

When aggressive behaviors are used in a relationship to control the other person, they lead to an unsafe, potentially abusive situation.

The person who is prone to selfish and unrestrained expressions of aggression may need to change how he thinks about his anger. St. Paul's admonition not to "give place to the devil" may be taken to mean not allowing anger to drag you back down into selfish aggression. We need to learn to think of aggression as a weakness we must overcome rather than as a right we deserve. It is important to state here that this pattern of behavior can be overcome with the guidance of a professional, who can help you learn new ways of expressing your frustration and also, possibly, uncover the underlying causes and pain that drive this aggression.

Finding healthy ways to handle anger and avoid aggression is important, not only to our personal relationships, but also to our spiritual state and our relationship with God. When we allow anger to deteriorate into aggression, when we allow ourselves the selfish indulgence of lashing out unkindly at a partner, we are betraying the central principle of Christianity (and of marriage): agape love. While it may be unavoidable to hurt our partners in this way at times because of our human weakness, if love is present, we will always feel a genuine sense of regret and repentance afterward.

Divine agape love means we will always be sensitive to our partner's needs, even at the very moment we are angry. If we aren't like this, if we let anger run wild, the relationship will suffer, just as it will suffer from any kind of uncontrolled selfishness. This is one way that marriage, that beautiful icon of the love between God and humanity, can be disfigured and God's good will for us thwarted: "For the wrath of man does not produce the righteousness of God" (James 1:20).

Selfish and unbridled expressions of aggression have the power to corrupt you to the very core of your being. They make your soul ugly and give it the flavor of hell (Matt. 5:21–25). They can lead to hypocrisy by blinding you to your own faults while you rage against those of your partner, setting yourself up as her judge. And they can harden your heart over time, slowly sucking the kindness from it and sucking the joy out of your relationship. Learn then, together as a united couple, to harness anger to your benefit and mingle it inseparably with love and kindness.

Communicating with each other in kindness is another powerful way to influence the quality of our relationships. Kindness is a commandment of God: "And be kind to one another, tenderhearted, forgiving one another, even as God in Christ forgave you. Therefore be imitators of God as dear children. And walk in love, as Christ also has loved us and given Himself for us" (Eph. 4:32—5:2).

Within a relationship so close and intense as marriage, it is common to feel the need to protect your individual rights against what you might see as the injustice of your partner. One way we do this is through teaching our partners a lesson. "Eye for eye, tooth for tooth" (Ex. 21:24) will keep my partner in check, will teach her to respect me. But as it has been observed, "An eye for an eye will leave the whole world blind."[28]

As Christians, we live in the New Covenant, not the Old. The Old taught us justice, but the New takes us beyond justice into mercy, compassion, and unconditional love. The two are not opposed, but justice lays the foundation for mercy. Thus did Christ teach us to turn the other cheek (Matt. 5:39). Turning the other cheek means you become a better, kinder, and more mature person, a person who is more Christlike.

You are responsible for your partner before God. There is no better way to nurture your partner and help her to grow as a person than by making your relationship one of kindness. In marriage, we need to create the secure environment of mutual love and kindness that makes turning the other cheek not only easier but a genuine pleasure. Consider the beautiful words of St. John Chrysostom:

> "Husbands love your wives just as Christ loved the Church" (Ephesians 5:25) . . . You have seen the amount of obedience necessary; now see the amount of love necessary. Do you want your wife to be obedient to you, as the Church is to Christ? Then be responsible for the same providential care of her, as Christ is of the Church. And even if it becomes necessary for you to give your life for her, yes, and even to endure and undergo suffering of any kind, do not refuse. Even though you undergo all this, you will never

---

28   Attributed to Mahatma Gandhi.

have done anything equal to what Christ has done. You are sac-rificing yourself for someone to whom you are already joined, but He offered Himself up for one who turned her back on Him and hated Him. In the same way, then, as He honored her by putting at His feet one who turned her back on Him, who hated, rejected, and disdained Him, as He accomplished this not with threats, or violence, or terror, or anything else like that, but through His untiring love; so also you should behave toward your wife. Even if you see her belittling you, or despising and mocking you, still you will be able to subject her to yourself, through affection, and kind-ness, and your great regard for her. There is no influence more powerful than the bond of love, especially for husband and wife. A servant can be taught submission through fear; but even he, if provoked too much, will soon seek his escape. But one's partner for life, the mother of one's children, the source of one's every joy, should never be fettered with fear and threats, but with love and patience. What kind of marriage can there be when the wife is afraid of her husband? What sort of satisfaction could a husband himself have, if he lives with his wife as if she were a slave, and not with a woman by her own free will? Suffer anything for her sake, but never disgrace her, for Christ never did this with the Church.[29]

The safe and secure environment in which love can flourish is also created when our words and actions are characterized by honesty and trust. Again, these are merely characteristics of a sincere Christian personality, but they are even more important within a marriage relationship. Remember that Christian mar-riage means that two individuals become one. They trust each other as they trust themselves. There is no human being that is closer to you than your partner, no human being to whom you make yourself so vulnerable. To be able to do that, and to enjoy

---

29   St. John Chrysostom, op. cit., pp. 46–47.

all the wonderful benefits that intimacy brings, you need to trust each other. And to trust each other, you need to be honest with each other.

Honesty is another way of speaking and acting that can have a profound influence on the quality of our relationships. We all know that honesty is a good thing. "Lying lips are an abomination to the Lord, / But he who shows faithfulness is acceptable to Him" (Prov. 12:22 [24 in OSB]). We especially value honesty in others, yet we sometimes give ourselves special-case permission to be dishonest. Christ called Himself, among other things, "the truth" (John 14:6). When we depart from truth, we are departing from Christ, to our own hurt and often also to the hurt of others. Lying leads to anxiety, stress, and worrying that you may be found out. This decreases the quality of your own life, and it can have a terrible effect on your relationship. Problems that are left in the dark fester and grow and send their groping, poisonous tentacles into many other parts of your relationship. Hiding your feelings can allow them to build up into very unhealthy gripes or feelings of being hurt.

On the other hand, honesty brings with it relief, peace, and security. You know exactly where you stand. You know you can always believe what your partner tells you, and you also know you don't have to convince him to believe what you say. In so many ways, being honest results in a much more peaceful life! Embrace honesty with all your being and say, as did the righteous Job, "My lips will not speak lawless things / Nor shall my soul practice wrongdoings. . . . Until the day I die, I will not put away my integrity from me" (Job 27:4, 5).

Honesty nurtures trust, one of the things that makes marriage so beautiful. But trust is a fragile thing. It follows the Humpty Dumpty rule: like an eggshell, once broken, it is very hard to put together again. It is certainly not impossible, but it is very hard. So it is wise to put all you have into preventing trust from being broken in the first place. Being honest may sometimes feel like it costs you a lot—perhaps it drags you into an argument, wounds your ego, or makes you look stupid. But all these things are resolved relatively easily and soon forgotten. Broken trust, on the other hand, is so much harder to rebuild. So count the cost and choose the least harmful path—that of honesty.

Gender Differences

In the next chapter we are going to consider the changing nature of gender roles in the modern marriage relationship, and we will see that there are differing theological views on the importance of gender. One thing that is not so controversial is that there are certain patterns of attitudes and behaviors that seem to characterize male and female approaches to relationships.

Every person is an individual, and many of the patterns described below can cross gender lines. While we suspect that most of what you will read will apply to the gender described, some of it may apply to a person of the opposite gender, and this is perfectly normal. What is most important, then, is that you understand your own and your partner's unique individual psyche. This kind of understanding can prevent an immense amount of trouble and heartache. As third-party observers of couples in trouble, we have seen just how easy it is for the kinds of common misunderstandings described below to snowball into major incidents and longstanding resentments. These not only detract from the joy of marriage and of life in general, but they can even lead to tragic consequences.

In our experience, both women and men share a common

complaint of not being understood and appreciated by the other. As we talk with women, we often find the root cause of this sense of being misunderstood is that they do not believe they are being heard by men; they believe men listen provisionally with the sole aim of providing solutions. When a woman feels this way over a prolonged period of time, she starts to share less and less about herself and slowly withdraws emotionally from the relationship. At the same time, men often complain that women are unappreciative of them—they do not believe women are proud of them, and this is evidenced by the women's attempts to help men improve. The reality often is that both men and women mistakenly believe that by responding in these ways to each other, they are providing the support the other needs.

The primary reason these complaints are common is that men and women are different and, as such, express themselves differently, deal with stress differently, and have differing needs. The kinds of traits we are talking about here are nicely explored in John Gray's popular book, *Men Are from Mars, Women Are from Venus*.[30] Consider the differences in how men and women deal with stress, their sense of self-worth, and communication, and see if you can recognize these patterns in your own personality and that of your partner.

Dealing with stress

When they're upset, men often prefer to be alone, to unwind and try to process the issue they are faced with prior to talking to anyone else about it. This is sometimes referred to as entering their cave. This may not necessarily be a physical place. Rather, it is engaging in an activity that shifts their attention away from the

---

30   John Gray, *Men Are from Mars, Women Are from Venus* (New York: HarperCollins, 2011).

issue at hand, such as watching a sports match or working on a project in the garage. Most men also prefer to handle problems on their own; they will rarely talk about a problem unless they need expert advice or wish to blame someone. To a man, speaking about problems is burdening another person unnecessarily. Therefore, whenever problems are discussed with men, they assume the person speaking to them either wants a solution from them or is blaming them. In both cases, they may provide advice and/or become defensive. For this reason, they assume the most caring response they can provide to their partner when a problem is being discussed is to offer a solution.

Women generally respond in the opposite way—they will usually want to talk when they are upset. By sharing their problems, women achieve closeness. A woman under stress is not immediately concerned with finding solutions to her problems, but rather seeks relief by expressing herself and being understood.

For a typical woman, the fact that her partner prefers time alone when he is faced with a problem can be misunderstood to mean that he is disconnecting from her or that he is excluding her from a certain area of his life. For men, a woman's reluctance to accept his advice when facing a problem can be translated as rejection.

Self-worth

A man's self-worth correlates with his ability to achieve results autonomously. To offer a man unsolicited advice is to make him feel you think he doesn't know what to do. For women, showing love to another means offering them help without being asked, as well as being available to hear and share the other's problems and concerns. A wife will want to provide any help she can in order to help her mate overcome whatever issue he is facing.

Unfortunately, this can backfire because he may understand her offer of help—a sincere expression of her love for him—as an attack on his capability as a man. A classic example of this is when a wife gives her husband directions while he's driving, and he translates this to mean that she believes he is incapable of reaching their destination alone, which makes him become defensive.

For women, sharing is of greater importance than the achievement of goals or the attainment of success. It is through sharing her problems and emotions that she achieves intimacy and closeness in relationships. Her sense of self-worth correlates with the condition of her relationships and her ability to be open and feel understood within those relationships.

Communication

Men and women also communicate differently. Understanding these differences can be a big step toward being able to translate each other's languages. Just as misunderstandings can cause a lot of heartache and pain, translating and understanding can bring about peace, joy, and closeness in the relationship. How do men and women tend to communicate?[31]

Men	Women
Men focus on one issue or task at a time.	Women can be thinking, feeling, and talking about multiple issues at the same time.

---

31   The following table is adapted from Gray, op. cit.

When a woman conveys feelings of unhappiness, a man often takes this to mean he has failed.	To fully express feelings, women assume poetic license to use various adjectives, exaggerations, metaphors, and generalizations; for example, when a woman says "never," it may not literally mean "never."
Men prefer to cope with stress by retreating into the isolation of their "cave." Here a man is usually unresponsive and unaware of his surroundings, since he is consumed by the issue at hand. He is usually only able to perform tasks that involve five percent of his brain power, so he can continue to process the problem with the remaining ninety-five percent. When he feels he has regained control of the situation and has a solution ready, then he will be ready to come out and pay attention to other matters again.	Women prefer to cope with stress by talking through the issue that troubles them with someone who is sympathetic and willing to listen.
Men come to feel better by reaching a solution.	Women come to feel better by talking through problems.
Sharing problems for men equates to placing the burden upon another (bad).	Sharing problems for women equates to love and trust (good).
Men tend to need to feel better, regain control, or resolve their own issues *prior to* helping or being available to others.	Women will often involve themselves in the problems of others *in order to* resolve their own issues and feel better.

For a couple to communicate effectively, they need to be aware that they are different and respect that difference. Although they may use the same words, those words often convey different meanings. The man needs to know that the more his wife feels unheard, the more issues she becomes upset about. She can also make it easier for him to hear her by reassuring him at the start of a conversation that she is not about to start blaming him for anything but simply wants him to listen.

It is often easier for both men and women to default to offering each other the kind of support they expect for themselves. However, successful relationships are ones where each person offers the other the form of support that is *needed*, not the one they themselves prefer to receive. Not only will the dynamics of the relationship work better, but the very act of understanding and accommodating yourself to your partner is in itself a powerful message of love and care. It tells your partner that she is important enough to you for you to invest your time and effort into understanding her and to change the way you do things to make her feel comfortable. This too is an opportunity for that wonderful, freely given, self-sacrificial agape love that is the epitome of sincere Christianity. Let us consider some of the ways this plays out in real life.

> » A man needs to be released to enter his cave when he is
> overwhelmed. The wife need not be anxious—he will
> surely return. For this to happen, though, a man often
> needs to reassure his wife that he will return, and that at
> a set agreed time there will be an opportunity to discuss
> whatever issue they are facing together. This assurance is
> crucial to preventing the woman from feeling neglected
> when the man enters his cave.

» A man needs to be approached as the solution to the problem rather than as being part of the problem. When this happens, a man is much more likely to be engaged and active in a successful outcome. But if he starts to believe he is a failure, he is likely to become disengaged, negative, and withdrawn.

» A woman needs to be heard and empathized with, not lectured, when facing a problem. It is critical that a man know that a woman will become frustrated, and at times feel insulted, if all she gets every time she shares a problem is a strategy or a solution. What she often wants from talking to her partner is connection and intimacy, not to be given a solution. If she needs advice, she will ask for it, but only if she knows she has been heard.

» Most importantly, both men and women need to accept that each is different from the other without judgment. By doing so, each person can appreciate those differences and grow in fondness for the other.

How well do you understand the differences between the ways men and women communicate? Below is a little role-play that portrays some of the common mistakes people make. Read through it and see if you can spot what the couple are doing wrong. Rupert and Cynthia are a fictional loving couple who have been married for just under a year. They have both worked very hard to build a life for themselves, and they are both very committed to their marriage, but sometimes they find that things just go terribly wrong for no apparent reason. As you read through the role-play, see if you can answer the questions below:

» What is each of them *really* trying to say, even if their words don't say it outright?

» How is each of them misunderstanding the other? What is going wrong?

» What would have been a better way to communicate what they wanted to say or to handle the situation?

To find out how well you understood the mechanics of communication going on here, there is another version of the same role-play in the appendix at the end of the book with a "translation."

Rupert and Cynthia Have an Argument

[Rupert walks in cheerfully, holding flowers behind his back.]

Rupert: Hi dear! Sorry I'm late—I got held up at the office by that new Japanese client. Never seen anyone who cares so much about details! It was "this is too small," and "that's too red," and "you didn't put enough of this in." I'd hate to be his wife, hey! Anyway, look. I'm really sorry, and I just got you a little something to show you how sorry I am . . .

[Proudly, he produces flowers from behind his back. Cynthia looks at him coldly and turns away without taking the flowers. Rupert continues, less certain of himself.]

Rupert: I, er . . . I had a lot of trouble choosing these, you know. Ummmm. You don't like them?

Cynthia: Rupert, sometimes I wonder if you still love me . . .

Rupert: Love you? Of course I love you, you silly woman! What do you think these flowers are for?

Cynthia: You never spend time with me anymore.

Rupert: What??? Come on, last Tuesday we had a lovely evening together.

Cynthia: *[giving a withering stare]* Most of the time, it's as if I'm not even there. You just ignore me. You're too tied up with your stupid job and your stupid Chinese friend.

Rupert: Number one, he's not my friend, he's a client—he pays for our lifestyle. And number two, he's not Chinese, he's Japanese. And—

Cynthia: *[cutting him off angrily]* I don't care if he's an Eskimo from Afghanistan—you don't love me the way you used to!

Rupert: I don't . . . What do you mean . . . Oh, I give up. This is pointless.

[Rupert turns and walks over to a chair, sits down and switches on the TV using a remote. His eyes are glued to the TV as the conversation continues.]

Cynthia: What do you think you're doing? You're not going to watch TV now?

Rupert: Come on, Cynthia, I'm tired and I really don't want to get into this now. We can sort it out tomorrow.

Cynthia: You're upset with me, aren't you?

Rupert: I'm not upset, I'm okay.

Cynthia: Yes, you are. You're just switching off.

Rupert: Look, I'm not upset. It's not a problem.

Cynthia: Not a problem? Not a problem??? You don't think we have a problem?

Rupert: I didn't say . . .

Cynthia: *[cutting him off]* How can you do this? How can you sit there and say we have no problem? Why do you think I'm upset? Why do you think you're so upset with me?

Rupert: Look, for the last time, I'm NOT upset. I'm fine. Now just leave me alone or I WILL get upset!

[An extremely tense minute passes . . .]

Rupert: *[taking his eyes off the TV at last]* Come and sit down. *[She sits next to him.]* Don't you know you're the most important thing in my whole life? Don't you know that making you happy is what matters the most to me? It's just that sometimes I don't know what to do to make you happy, and I make mistakes. You've gotta help me out.

Cynthia: Look, I'm sorry, Rupert. I know you've had a hard day. I really appreciate how hard you work for us both. And I really appreciate that you went out of your way to get those flowers for me. You're a good husband. But if I don't blow off steam with you, who can I blow it off with? My mother?

Rupert and Cynthia's little episode is not just an example of how couples often run into misunderstandings; it's also a classic example of a cycle that many couples fall into. It's called a *pursue–withdraw cycle*. Almost all relationships begin in a state where both individuals are pursuing each other. Whenever the slightest problem happens, both rush in to fix it and help the other feel better.

However, over time a couple can find themselves in a pursue–withdraw state without realizing it. This is where one partner becomes aware of the other's withdrawal or feelings of hurt and pursues them in order to reconnect and heal the relationship. The other reacts to being so pursued by feeling bombarded, trapped, or even controlled, so they withdraw further. The more the one pursues, the more the other withdraws. The couple will alternate roles as time passes.

Cynthia and Rupert were able to reconnect after pausing a

moment and reflecting. However, for many couples this cycle goes on for much longer, and over time both can ultimately come to rest in a withdrawn state, having checked out emotionally from the relationship.

The reality is, at any given time, there is usually one person trying to pursue the other and repair the relationship. Over time each of the members of the couple takes that role at some point. However, because the withdrawing partner is stuck in his state, he fails to see the pursuing partner's attempts to heal the relationship and show her love and affection.

If each person can come to see that the pattern of the cycle, and not their partner, is the enemy, they can then start to recognize when each person is pursuing the other. In doing so, they can come to understand that this pursuit is actually an expression of their love for each other and of the value the relationship holds for them.

Commitment

If all this seems to you like hard work, that probably means you have understood the reality of marriage. Fr. Joseph Purpura of the Antiochian Orthodox Church in North America wrote:

> When I was a parish priest, I was often asked, during the course of pre-marital counseling, what it would take to have a long and successful marriage. I would often send these couples to spend some time with some of the elderly couples of the parish who had been married for fifty or more years. I would then ask upon their return, "what did they say?" I always heard a similar answer: "they said they worked at making their marriage work," "they only thought of making it work, no matter how bad it got," "it was

not always this good, there were rough times and we had to really work at it."[32]

Marriage *is* hard work, but it is full of joy and delight. Just as raising a child is hard work yet a joy and delight beyond words, so is marriage, the prelude to children. One of the things that make it so precious is its unconditional commitment. As we saw in the last chapter, there is something inexpressibly life-affirming and fulfilling about being able to give yourself totally to another person and to have him entrust himself totally to you.

Life is really just slow death if it has no purpose, no vocation. We often think of priesthood when we use the term *vocation*, but as Fr. Alexander Schmemann points out,[33] we must all have a vocation, priest or layperson, married or single: "The meaning, the essence and the end of all vocation is the mystery of Christ and the Church."

You are to love and serve your partner the same way a priest loves and serves the Church, the way Christ loves and serves humanity. Marriage is one of the things that allows us to live out this vocation, giving it a concrete, visible target. Thus, through marriage, we find meaning and purpose for our lives—not in a selfish and melodramatic overdependence on another human being, but in the conscious imitation of Christ's self-sacrificial, unconditional, and all-enduring love.

This is a vocation that demands the rest of our lives and a commitment to see it through, no matter what. As a married couple, you and your partner have something that is very special—in fact, unique. You get to share things with each other that no one else

---

32   Fr. Joseph Purpura, *The Angel's Voice Newsletter* 2, no. 3.
33   Fr. Alexander Schmemann, *For the Life of the World* (Crestwood, NY: St. Vladimir's Seminary Press, 1973), p. 94.

in the world gets to share. That private intimacy is one of the things that makes marriage so fulfilling and teaches us about the nature of love, so it is something to treasure and protect.

This great gift comes with great responsibility. You become responsible for your partner as well as yourself. While it is true that we can never evade our own responsibility for our own actions (it didn't work for Adam and Eve in the Garden, nor ever since), we are responsible for the influence we have on others. So, while you will never be able to say, "My partner made me do it," neither will you ever be able to say, "I had nothing to do with my partner's sin."

We find here two complementary principles that together reflect another aspect of self-giving agape love. On the one hand, we should always take full responsibility for our own actions rather than blaming others. No one forces you to do anything, not even God, so even if your partner has a bad influence on you, you alone are the final decision-maker. It is a sign of maturity to be able to take responsibility for one's own actions.

On the other hand, you should feel responsible to do all you can to help and support your partner in doing the right thing. While your influence can never take away his free choice, it can be a powerful force that he can harness and use to his benefit. If your partner is unhappy because of something you have said or done, the mature thing to do is to take responsibility for your role in the matter and do what is necessary to fix it, even at your own cost. In the end, it is not really a cost to you, since by making your partner happy, you are really making yourself happy.

This is the work of a lifetime, and it requires liberal doses of patience. But fortunately, we have a whole lifetime to work on ourselves. Young couples sometimes get quite anxious when things go wrong early in their life together. Remember that you are not the first couple to go through this process, nor will you be the last. It is a general principle in life that time can change many things. The problem that seems so big and impossible to solve today will probably be fixed up by tomorrow (or next week). What is more, the load is no longer one you must carry alone but one that is shared between the two of you. Today it may be you who must be patient with your partner; tomorrow the roles may be reversed. Remember that moving passage from Ecclesiastes?

> Two are better than one
> Because they have a good reward for their labor.
> For if they fall, one will lift up his companion.
> But woe to him who is alone when he falls,
> For there is not a second one to help him up!
> If two lie down together, both stay warm,
> But how can one stay warm alone?
> If one is added strength, two will stand before him,
> And a threefold cord is not quickly broken. (Eccl. 4:9–12)

We often advise people to let the third strand in that three-fold cord, the strand that binds and strengthens the other two, be Christ. His unlimited patience with each of us, despite our betrayals, weaknesses, and sins, is enough to inspire and empower anyone to be patient with her spouse for the whole of their lives. Indeed, without this divine grace, we are probably incapable of practicing the kind of patience a marriage needs. Let your patience therefore be founded and grounded in the divine agape love that fills our hearts when we are united with Christ. This is the love that "bears all things, believes all things, hopes all things, [and] endures all things" (1 Cor. 13:7). This is the kind of patience that makes us better and nobler people.

Patience comes to the surface especially when your partner is going through a major difficulty. Serious illness, unemployment, bereavement, and mid-life crisis are all examples of times when one partner needs to be patient with the other. In these situations, such patience is a truly beautiful image of divine, unselfish love. How inspiring to meet a husband who has given up his work to care for his wife, ailing with cancer! How moving to see the wife smiling and staying optimistic through her husband's bout of depression! These people are all the more admirable and worthy because they refused the easy option—to cut and run when things got difficult. This is the kind of commitment all of us hope to find in our partners, and we consider ourselves blessed to be in such a relationship. But Christ teaches us not to seek to be so loved, but to be the kind of person who practices such love.

Reflection Questions on Living Together in Christ

» What does it mean to you to "invite Christ to live in your home every day"?

» How are you going to find the right balance between your own personal time with God and the many demands of marriage and family life? Do you have a plan?

» What spiritual activities are you going to commit to doing together? Prayer? Bible reading? Fasting? Having confession and communion? Serving? What else?

» Do you think it is practical to expect that you will never go to bed angry with each other? How might your spiritual practices facilitate a better relationship between you?

Reflection Questions on Wise Counsel

» How do we acquire wisdom?

» How can you know when it is time to seek counsel from a third party?

» How do you go about choosing whom to consult when you need counsel?

» What are the warning signs that the person who is counseling you is not really going to improve things and may even make things worse?

Reflection Questions on the Importance of Intentions

» What is *conception of intention,* and why is it such an important aspect of any relationship?

» How often do you make assumptions about your partner's intentions that turn out to be misplaced? How do you both deal with it when this happens?

» What is your chief love language, and what is that of your partner? Do you accommodate your behavior toward your partner to his or her preferred love language?

Reflection Questions on How to Be United

» What does the concept of marital unity mean to you? What does it look like?

» What does it mean to own everything together? How does this work in practice?

» Identify some activities you and your partner can enjoy doing *together.* How might you make sure you always have time for these, no matter how busy your lives become?

» Describe a situation or an experience purely from your partner's point of view, rather than your own. Ask your partner to tell you how accurately you managed to walk in his or her shoes.

» How are you going to go about making decisions in your married life? What is the process going to look like? What part will each of you play?

» What issues are there in your lives, both present and future, that might potentially drive you apart?
» How can you guard against others interfering in your relationship when either one or both of you does not want them to?

Reflection Questions on Personalities in Marriage

» How do you communicate feelings within your relationship? Do you think your current emotional communication patterns are effective, or would you like them to be different in some way?
» What differences have you identified in each other that might potentially be a problem?
» What weaknesses can you identify in yourself that are complemented by strengths in your partner?
» Are you in a relationship with an opposite personality type?
   ◊ If so, what attracted you to this person initially?
   ◊ Do you still find those characteristics attractive? If not, what has changed? At what point did you start to notice this change?
   ◊ What do you believe would be the ideal way of communicating with your partner, considering the differences in your personality types?
» Are you in a relationship with the same personality type?
   ◊ If so, what things do you have in common that you cherish?
   ◊ How do you think you can benefit from your similarities?
   ◊ How do you think your relationship can benefit from dealing with people of other personality types?

Reflection Questions on the Power of Words

» What type of words have you been speaking to your partner? Are they words that connect or disconnect you?

» Can you think of a time when you spoke words that caused
division between you and a time that you spoke words
of peace? What were the differences between the two
incidents?

» Have you been flinging put-downs toward someone? Take a
moment to consider what it would be like for them to be on
the receiving end of your criticism. How else can you get
your message across without inflicting pain?

» How easy do you think it is for people to misunderstand
what others say to them? How could you limit the damage
caused by misunderstandings?

» Try this exercise: get your partner to tell you about something for three full minutes. You must then repeat back as
much as you can remember of what he or she said for one
full minute. How much did you actually comprehend and
retain of what he or she said? How did it make your
partner feel?

Reflection Questions on the Way We Speak and Act

» What does this verse mean to you: "Let every man be swift
to hear, slow to speak, slow to wrath" (James 1:19)? How
might it apply in your relationship?

» Do you treat your partner with more kindness and courtesy
than you do friends or strangers, or with less? How important is it to say little things like "please" and "thank you,"
and to open doors for each other?

» How often do you perform acts of kindness for your partner
without being asked?

» When was the last time you received a genuine compliment? How did it make you feel?

» How do you think paying your partner more compliments would affect your relationship?

» How important are honesty and truth in your relationship? What price are you willing to pay to preserve them?

Reflection Questions on Gender Differences

» If there is a problem that affects both partners, how do you go about resolving it? Do you do this in a way that respects the needs of both the man and the woman? If not, what do you think can be done differently?

» Have there been times when you have been confused by your partner's reaction to problems? How have you, as a couple, dealt with this situation?

» Think of an example where one of you was saying one thing, but the other understood something else completely. How did you deal with that situation? What might be the best way to deal with it?

» If you are a man:
  ◊ How do you normally deal with problems?
  ◊ How does your partner normally react to your coping strategies?
  ◊ How have you dealt with your partner's emotional expressions in the past?

» If you are a woman:
  ◊ What is it like for you when your partner closes in on himself or does not share information about his problems with you?
  ◊ How have you interpreted this behavior in the past, and how would you understand it now?

Reflection Questions on Commitment

> » In what ways is your relationship with your partner a *vocation* to you?
>
> » Commitment in marriage is a reflection of the commitment between God and humanity. In what ways are the two alike?
>
> » How do you both benefit from being committed to each other?
>
> » In what ways are you responsible for your partner, and in what ways are you responsible for yourself?
>
> » In what ways could you and your partner regularly renew and celebrate your commitment to each other?

CHAPTER FIVE

TWONESS AND ONENESS

Some Important Issues

Who will find a courageous wife?
For such a one is more valuable than precious
  stones.
"Many daughters acquire riches; many do mighty
  things,
But you excel and surpass all."

(PROVERBS 31:10, 28)

Let the husband render to his wife the affection
due her, and likewise also the wife to her husband.
The wife does not have authority over her own
body, but the husband does. And likewise the hus-
band does not have authority over his own body,
but the wife does.

(1 CORINTHIANS 7:3–4)

WE HAVE LOOKED AT THE TIMELESS MYSTERY OF marriage, its meaning, its beauty, and its place in the overall scheme of Christian salvation. We have seen how, from the earliest centuries of Christianity, marriage was blessed and sanctified by the Holy Spirit through the Church and thus drawn up into the circle of divine love, transformed and transfigured into a vivid and living icon of the relationship between God and humanity. All this is just as relevant and just as important in the twenty-first century as it was in the first.

We have also tried to bring to bear the best wisdom we have today from the psychological sciences to paint a picture of how to go about creating, maintaining, and enjoying a fruitful and fulfilling marriage relationship. But while the twenty-first century has brought with it excellent insights into how relationships work, it has also brought with it a number of challenges that first-century Christians—and perhaps even our grandparents—may not have found so important or even been aware of. Today, however, these issues have the potential to make or break a marriage. In this section we will address some of these topics and try to apply the ancient and timeless basic principles of Christian marriage to some of today's most prominent issues.

Male and Female

We considered above the differences between the ways men and women communicate and how those differences can lead to serious misunderstandings and clashes if they are not understood and respected. In this section, we would like to reflect in a broader way upon how expectations of men and women have changed in recent times and try to provide some guidance on how to minimize the anxiety and uncertainty to which this change in gender expectations has given rise.

One major change has been the move toward equality between the genders. In the public sphere, that equality has translated into equality of educational and career opportunities, salaries, political representation, and so on. But how has it translated in the private sphere of the home? It is very likely that the roles your parents played in their marriage, and almost certainly those played by your grandparents, were quite different from the roles you will end up playing in your marriage.

Gone are the days when the wife was expected to stay at home, do the housework, and care for the children, while the husband had to go out and earn a living to support the family and could just come home and put his feet up. Unless you and your partner understand the flexibility that has come to characterize gender roles today, there will be quite a danger of discontentment and resentment in the relationship.

As we have seen above, your relationship ought to be built above all upon a foundation of Christian agape love—unselfish, unconditional, and joyfully giving. The modern trend toward more flexible gender roles in marriage is completely in harmony with this principle, but it will need some thought and effort from you both if you are to apply it successfully.

The social trends have been reflected in philosophical circles, where feminist philosophy of various stripes has been popular for many decades now. Feminism seeks to examine how being a human in the world differs for men and women, whether in terms of our physical, emotional, psychological, or even spiritual attitudes, and our ways of engaging with the world in which we live. These gender differences result not only from how we see ourselves, but also from how society treats people differently according to their gender.

For those who are interested in the theological side of the matter, there is a fascinating discussion going on today in Orthodox Christian circles about how relevant our gender is to who we are as human beings in the image of God. "So God made man;

in the image of God He made him; male and female He made them" (Gen. 1:27). But what does this tell us about the importance of gender to who we are?

Notice that *both* male and female are made in the image of God. Theologians such as Fr. Thomas Hopko and Fr. John Behr[34] have argued that our gender in fact reflects different aspects of God. Of course, God is neither male nor female Himself, since He transcends gender,[35] but perhaps certain aspects of God's nature are more fully reflected in maleness, while others are more fully reflected in femaleness? The incarnate Word of God, Jesus Christ, certainly lived His life as a male human being and not as a female, but we also find God described in somewhat feminine language, as a mother for example (see Deut. 32:11; Is. 66:13).

Some theologians, like Valerie Karras,[36] have argued that the crucial thing about humans is that they are created in the image of God, and that gender is a merely incidental thing. It is a consequence of our fallen state, but not something that defines

---

34 Thanks to Fr. John for kindly providing the authors with a copy of this article and others on this topic. See Fr. John Behr, "A Note on the Ontology of Gender," *St. Vladimir's Theological Quarterly* 42, no. 3–4 (1998): pp. 363–72.

35 In English we commonly use the masculine pronoun for God, but the Bible in the original languages of Hebrew and Greek also uses the feminine construction of God where it is grammatically appropriate, such as when referring to the Holy Spirit. Perhaps the most accurate usage would be to invent a completely unique pronoun for God that is neither male nor female, rather than argue over whether we should refer to God as "He" or "She" (but certainly not "It"!).

36 See Valerie A. Karras, "Patristic Views on the Ontology of Gender," in *Personhood: Orthodox Christianity and the Connection Between Body, Mind, and Soul*, ed. John T. Chirban (Westport: Praeger Publishers, 1996), pp. 113–19.

us. Thus the human soul itself and alone is seen as being without gender, and we will exist in the heavenly state without gender—"There is neither male nor female; for you are all one in Christ Jesus" (Gal. 3:28).

This is not a question we need to explore in detail here, but it may be worth discussing with your partner how important you think gender is to who you are and how you think, feel, and behave. It may have significant consequences for the roles you expect of each other in the relationship.

Consider this question: "What do men and women want from their spouses?" Answers to this question will of course vary widely from person to person. Most people begin thinking about this question in terms of, "What do I want?" but find it much harder to deal with in terms of, "Am I providing my spouse with what he or she wants?" Here are some observations from Fr. Gabriel Yassa, a Coptic parish priest who served engaged and married couples for many years. How many of these needs apply to you and to your partner?

Male Needs

- » A woman who can see and value the greatness in him.
- » A woman who is able to support and fuel his dreams. He doesn't need her to shatter his wonderful plans but to encourage or very gently discourage.
- » A woman who is able to strengthen and complete his weakness. Inside every big man is a small child who only appears when the environment is safe and he feels secure enough to reveal this side of himself. She needs to take care not to take advantage of his vulnerability.

Female Needs

- » A man who is emotionally available when she needs him. He doesn't have to do much, just be there when needed. As she thinks out loud, she needs him to be empathically present and listen to her. He needs to allow these conversations to be about her concerns, not redirect them to his own concerns.
- » A man who provides her with reassurance and self-worth. A man who tells her "I love you," repeated at least three times a day, who praises her appearance and her contributions to the home, who does not look at other women.
- » A man who can provide security rather than unpredictability and chaos. He never threatens.
- » A man who can provide attention and affection and give her big hugs when she needs them.

Do these needs reflect your own? Do they reflect the needs of your partner? Or are your respective needs different from those above? While they represent perhaps a common pattern in what people need in marriage, there will almost certainly be individual cases in which they will differ significantly. Problems arise when we make faulty assumptions about our partner's needs. It is important to emphasize the need for mutual understanding, acceptance, and accommodation of your partner's attitudes toward gender roles.

Intimacy and Sexuality

Attitudes toward talking about sexuality have evolved and changed significantly through the centuries. The very fact that an Orthodox Christian book about marriage contains a frank discussion of sexuality is something that would have shocked and perhaps offended many people fifty years ago. But we believe that the modern honesty and openness about sexuality is in fact a good thing and more in keeping with the honesty and truth of the Gospel—and the practice of the ancient Christian Church—than is the attitude of pretending it doesn't exist.

It also reflects the principle we discussed in the introduction: that our faith ought to permeate every aspect of our lives without exception, rather than dividing our lives up into isolated categories of sacred and secular. The Holy Spirit dwells with us in the bedroom just as much as He does in the Church, although of course we engage in rather different activities in those two places. And just as attitudes to talking about sexuality have changed over time, so also have attitudes toward sexuality itself changed. So to begin, we will briefly consider how early Christians thought about sexuality.

The first Christians did not of course emerge out of nowhere. They came to Christ bringing with them their own cultural attitudes and morals. Many of them were Jewish and were quite familiar with the Old Testament scriptures. There they read that the relationship between God and humans was often compared to that between a husband and wife, including not only ideals like loyalty and devotion, but also sexuality. They did not blush when they read the rather explicit sexual language of *Song of Songs* in the Bible but understood it to be employing a natural part of human life to portray the spiritual life. The analogy of marriage also turns up in Ezekiel 16 and in the whole Book of Hosea, although with a somewhat less happy ending due to sexual infidelity.

This use of sexuality as an analogy of spirituality continues in the New Testament, with the analogies in Ephesians 5 and the

"Bride of Christ" in the Book of Revelation, and there are certainly analogies between the union of a husband and wife and the union of Jesus and the human being in the Eucharist. In both cases, two become one.

The ancient Church Fathers not only discuss openly biblical passages such as those cited above, but they sometimes engage in frank explorations and reflections upon the role and meaning of sexuality in human life. For example, St. Gregory of Nyssa (fourth century) expresses characteristically measured opinions in his writings about the relationship between sexuality and rationality, how rationality identifies us as the divine image of God, while sexuality identifies us as one with the animal world. We are "rational animals" by our very nature, such that both our rationality and our sexuality are good creations of God, both liable to corruption in the Fall of humanity, and both redeemable in Christ.[37]

What is more, the ancient mysteries of the Church all involve a physical aspect, whether it be having your body immersed in water, being anointed with oil, or eating and drinking. And we believe the resurrected heavenly state to be a physical state, albeit a transformed physical state. The phrase, "we look for the resurrection of the body," is found in nearly all Orthodox baptismal creeds. The message is quite clear: the body—and its functions, including sexuality—is a good and holy thing that participates with the mind and spirit in the whole of the Christian journey. Human sexuality, when it is practiced within marriage, is a living metaphor for the unity of the human soul with God.

In direct contradiction to this attitude were the beliefs found

---

37   Fr. John Behr, "The Rational Animal: A Rereading of Gregory of Nyssa's *De Hominis Opificio," Journal of Early Christian Studies* 7, no. 2 (1999): pp. 219–47.

in many pagan cultures and most clearly illustrated by a religious movement called gnosticism that was thriving in the earliest centuries of Christianity. Roughly speaking, gnostics believed that all that is physical is evil, and all that is spiritual is good. Sexuality, therefore, being physical, must be evil and must therefore at most be tolerated in order to procreate. Otherwise it is something to be eradicated from our lives altogether.[38] This kind of attitude is also to be found in various forms in some strands of Greek philosophy, most notably the Stoicism and Neo-Platonism that heavily influenced many of the ancient Church Fathers, especially of the Alexandrian school.

We do find some views expressed by the ancient Christians that lean toward this negative kind of attitude toward sexuality. St. Paul somewhat grudgingly acknowledges that sex can be a motivation for a person to marry (1 Cor. 7:1–9). And a number of the ancient Fathers considered sexuality as being intended chiefly for procreation. Some even suggested that the spiritual couple ought to engage in sex only when seeking to have children but not at any other time.[39] For example, St. Justin Martyr, in the middle of the second century, defends the morality of Christians against pagan accusations of loose morals by stating, "But whether we marry, it is only that we may bring up children; or

---

38 Note that this motivation for celibacy is very different from that which motivates the Christian celibate, whether monk, nun, or consecrated servant. These Christians do not eliminate sexuality but transcend it, seeing the human act as being an icon of a spiritual reality and choosing to bypass it to jump directly to the reality it signifies. They do not do this because sexuality or the physical body is evil but acknowledge that they are good steps toward a higher goal.

39 An attitude reflected in the Roman Catholic Church's modern views on contraception; see below.

whether we decline marriage, we live continently."[40] St. Clement of Alexandria, writing at the end of the second century, advises, "To such a spiritual man, after conception, his wife is as a sister and is treated as if of the same father."[41]

But overall, Orthodox Christianity today teaches a healthy attitude to sexuality. Our bodies are good, and the functions with which God endowed them are also good. This includes sexuality, which we see as a holy and blessed gift from God, intended to help us experience love more fully. God did not create anything that was evil. As we noted earlier, the command to "be fruitful and multiply" was given to Adam and Eve *before* the Fall and was thus part of their paradisiacal state. It was the *pain* of childbirth that resulted from the Fall, not reproduction itself. Indeed, sanctified in marriage and thus used as it was intended, sexuality becomes an opportunity for the practice of unselfish, self-sacrificial love. It is an embodiment, a living out of the spiritual principle of escaping the shackles of the ego and being focused on the other. This is the very heart of divine agape love.

As in life generally, in sexuality, "It is more blessed to give than to receive" (Acts 20:35). Each partner ought to seek the pleasure and happiness of the other. If this happens, then both will enjoy a fulfilling sex life that brings them closer together emotionally and spiritually. The unselfish giving we practice in daily life and in big decisions is continuous with unselfish giving in the bedroom.

St. Paul goes so far as to tell the married that they must no longer consider their bodies as being their own but as belonging to their spouses: "The wife does not have authority over her own body, but the husband *does*. And likewise the husband does not

---

40   St. Justin Martyr, "First Apology," in Ante-Nicene Fathers, 1:172.

41   St. Clement of Alexandria, "Stromata," in Ante-Nicene Fathers, 2:503.

have authority over his own body, but the wife *does*" (1 Cor. 7:4).[42] Again, this must be understood not in the context of political power struggles between the two but of *voluntary* self-giving and submission. The authority over the body is not surrendered under duress and against the will but willingly, joyfully, and lovingly.

Where there is a giver, there is a receiver, and the joy of the giver in giving is increased by the joy of the receiver who receives that gift. Just as there is divine love in the joy your partner experiences when you give her an unexpected gift or cook his favorite meal, so also there is divine love in the giving of sexual pleasure. Here there is no need and no room for the guilt and shame that some cultures have attached to sexuality generally. That kind of attitude can be seen to be a denial of the goodness and the love of God, and it certainly has no place in a genuinely Christian marriage.

But this healthy attitude must not be mistaken for promiscuity, for it is always balanced by the principle of self-restraint. Sexuality is good *if* it is used the right way, as a means to growing in divine love. But if it is *abused*, it becomes not a blessing but a curse in our lives, corrupting us and spoiling the image of the God of love in us.

The more sexually conservative ancient Fathers had a point. There is more to their negative attitudes toward sex than just denying the physical. The goal of asceticism is to find the right balance in life. Asceticism is also a part of our Christian life, and it is even more necessary in our modern culture, which promotes an unhealthy imbalance. Consumers today are encouraged to binge out, to indulge themselves, to take far more than they really need of everything because, of course, that sells more products and is good for the economy. Whatever your product may

---

42   These words are repeated to the couple in the Coptic rite of marriage.

be—food, clothing, cars, or chocolates—you will sell a lot more of it by making it "sexy." The sad side effect of this trend has been to create a culture and a widespread mindset where sex plays a much bigger role than it deserves and occupies an unhealthy, disproportionately large place in our thinking.

When sex acquires this over-importance, it begins to be dangerous, and Paradise is lost. Sex then no longer leads to the unselfish self-sacrifice and self-giving which is the image of God. Instead it leads to addiction, enslavement by the passions, and a focus on satisfying one's own desires, even at the cost of others, as an overriding motivation in life. The Christian understands the purpose of life not as merely indulging one's base desires and instincts—as if we were nothing but animals—but rising above those instincts, sanctifying them by making them conform to the principles of divine agape love, making them outward-looking and unselfish.

Eros must be tamed by agape. Overcoming such self-centeredness is crucial to true Christian life. In fact, if the goal of Christian life is to return to the image of God, to live again in the state of Paradise, then the modern obsession with sex is clearly a step in the wrong direction. Seen from this perspective, marriage is a step toward normalizing sex: baptizing it, sanctifying it, and restoring it to the role and nature it was originally created to have. It is only in this sanctified state that sex can truly fulfill its purpose in us without causing damage along the way. Ideally, then, Christian marriage helps us to tame sex and bring it under control so that it may serve us rather than enslave us.

And so, even within marriage, Orthodox Christian couples are encouraged to practice times of fasting from sex. The goal is the same as that of fasting from food: to put it in its proper place and prevent it from ruling you. St. Paul taught that this kind of fasting must be practiced within the confines of divine love. For example, it must not be enforced by one partner upon the other, but should only be by mutual consent and with the goal of giving oneself to prayer and fasting (1 Cor. 7:5), mastering the fallen passions, and drawing nearer to God and to a healed state.

This reasoning lies behind other restrictions on our sex lives. Sex before marriage is harmful because it unites you with someone who may not end up being your spouse. Until you are married, there is always the chance that the relationship may not work out and that you may end up marrying someone else. To engage in this most intimate of acts with someone other than your spouse is a betrayal of the love and unity of which we have spoken. This also applies to engaging in sexual experiences with someone other than your spouse after you are married.

Within marriage itself, the overriding principle of divine love means that sexual activity must always be by mutual consent. It is possible for rape to occur within marriage, and it is just as horrible a violation of divine love as the rape of a stranger. Christian marriage leads us away from these kinds of perversions of the beautiful gift of God and back into the great good for which that gift was always intended, by restoring it as an act of self-giving, outward-looking, other-focused agape love.

On a more practical level, experience has taught us that sexuality is all too often the cause of marital discord and sadness and may even contribute to marriages breaking down altogether. At the heart of the matter is the concept of *intimacy*. To be intimate is to be close or to share your most private or personal feelings or information with another. In marriage, intimacy concerns a number of areas: emotional, spiritual, intellectual, sexual, recreational, and others. It is important to remember that intimacy is not an end goal in itself but rather a means to a deeper eternal goal and a journey that lasts throughout your marriage.

One of the reasons sexuality can be so problematic is that there are many myths about sexual intimacy in marriage. These include the idea that sexual intimacy is only a physical duty in marriage, that intimacy is an evil and sinful thing (as the gnostics believed), that it is a need mostly of husbands and that women just have to comply, and that it is the most important thing in a marriage. There are many, many more myths that have confused and polluted many people's beliefs, expectations, and experiences of sexual intimacy in marriage. Many couples may need to identify issues that could hinder their ability to have a healthy intimate relationship and consider their own existing sexual fears, ideas, and irrational beliefs accumulated throughout their lives, so that they can address them and move toward a healthier, blessed intimacy.

The reality is that *everything* that happens in a marriage has an impact on the sexual intimacy between a couple. Many factors can influence the ability to be intimate. Intimacy does not happen in a vacuum, so never underestimate the importance of having a healthy spiritual, intellectual, social, and recreational relationship with each other. Personal doubts are a major obstacle. You both need to overcome your shyness and feel free to talk about everything related to intimacy openly and honestly with one another. Body and self-image also play a crucial role in the success or failure of intimacy within marriage. It is therefore critical that a couple use positive praise and words of affirmation, not put-downs or criticisms, when communicating with one another.

Like communication and coping with stress, sexual intimacy is an area where men and women differ. These differences need to be considered and talked about honestly within a marriage. One such difference is that for men, generally, sexual intimacy leads to emotional intimacy. That is why, for example, a husband may feel quite comfortable in approaching his wife and initiating sexual intimacy after an argument or without much conversation.

But for a woman, this may feel uncomfortable because, for her, things go in the opposite direction: emotional intimacy is needed first, and it is this that leads to sexual intimacy. This difference causes many issues between husbands and wives, because they are unaware of the nature of each other's progression between emotional and sexual intimacy. Once a couple understands this progression, they are much more likely to achieve both emotional and sexual intimacy within their relationship.

Four specific obstacles to intimacy are worth highlighting, since they are commonly seen in modern marriages and often inflict havoc upon people's lives. The first is the prevalent cultural attitude of "try before you buy": premarital sex. As mentioned above, it is a betrayal of the significance of marriage and results in guilt and shame plaguing the relationship, even after marriage. Not only is it against the Christian understanding of marriage, statistics gathered by US Attorney Legal Services show that living together before getting married does not accomplish the goal that couples think it will. A couple that does not live together prior to getting married has a 20 percent chance of being divorced within five years. If the couple has lived together beforehand, that number jumps to 49 percent.[43]

Second is the destruction caused by pornography. Porn occurs in a fictional world with fictional characters, and it creates a set of expectations about body image and about sex in marriage that are quite literally impossible to fulfill in the real world. It sets a person up for disappointment, pulls couples apart from each other

---

43   U.S. Attorney Legal Services, "Divorce Statistics—Divorce Rates," http://www.usattorneylegalservices.com/divorce-statistics.html, April 2015.

sexually, and pollutes the regular viewer's mind with images and desires that are not in harmony with the kind of unselfish holy love that should characterize a Christian marital relationship.

Third is unresolved discontentment. When a person is not content with the level of intimacy in the marriage, he may resort to extramarital fantasies, affairs, what-ifs, and regrets. Comparing your partner to others, real or fictional, is not only unfair but a major contributor to these kinds of harmful behavior. It prevents you from seeing and appreciating your partner's good qualities and focuses your attention instead on her shortcomings. Inevitably, there is a resulting negative impact on the emotional intimacy between you and on your feelings of connectedness to one another.

And fourthly, it is worth emphasizing that our natural tendency to selfishness works against intimacy. Remember that true intimacy is about giving, not receiving, whereas the media and popular culture today tie physical intimacy to fulfilling one's own desires and pleasures. Selfishness is a dead end when it comes to intimacy. It frustrates the very thing it yearns for and strives to attain. Intimacy works *because* it takes us out of ourselves, whereas selfishness traps us within ourselves and renders us incapable of experiencing what it really means to be one with another.

Contraception and Abortion

Is it acceptable for a Christian couple to engage in sex without the goal of having a child? In other words, is contraception allowed in the Orthodox Church? It is widely known that the Roman Catholic Church has generally taken a strong stand against any form of artificial contraception,[44] but this is not so with Orthodox Christianity.

---

44   The Roman Catholic position on contraception is in fact a subtle and

The Roman Catholic position flows from that ancient view that sex can only be lawfully engaged in for procreation but is otherwise a kind of giving in to lust. As we have by now seen, in the Orthodox Christian understanding of marriage, sex serves a number of purposes, not just one.

It may be argued that procreation is no longer even the chief goal. Meyendorff points out that while in the Old Testament, procreation was so important that even sex outside marriage—say, with a concubine—was sometimes justified, in the New Testament there is a shift to a focus on eternal life rather than reproducing life here on earth. He notes, "Not a single New Testament text mentioning marriage points to procreation as its justification or goal."[45]

In addition to bringing children into the world, sex also serves as an expression of unselfish, giving love that binds the couple together and as a protection—when practiced within a loving marriage relationship—against the selfish abuse of the gift of sex. There is nothing that says that all three purposes of sex must be involved in *every* sexual act the couple shares. While it may be ideal for all three to be there, there will clearly be times when that is not possible (such as after the woman is no longer fertile due to age).

In the same way, eating food serves both the purposes of nourishing our bodies and of giving us an enjoyment through which we experience the generous love of God and for which we thank Him. Eating a chocolate involves the second purpose, but not the first, and that is fine. When we abstain from food for periods of

---

nuanced one and not as simple as it is sometimes made out to be in public discussions. Nonetheless, it does differ significantly from the common (though not universal) position of Orthodox Churches.

45 Meyendorff, op. cit., p. 13.

time while fasting, it is not because eating is evil but because that abstinence serves to help us progress spiritually and come closer to God. The same may be said of sexuality.

In the passage we mentioned earlier, where St. Paul tells the married couple that their bodies do not belong to themselves but to their spouses, he says, "Do not deprive one another except with consent for a time, that you may give yourselves to fasting and prayer; and come together again so that Satan does not tempt you because of your lack of self-control" (1 Cor. 7:2–5).

The couple abstain from sex not because they do not plan to have children but in order to focus on prayer and fasting. Sex is resumed not in order to have children but in order to satisfy desires that might otherwise drive one to seek satisfaction in harmful ways. The assumption that sex is only for procreation does not seem to be in St. Paul's mind at all.

What is more, modern Orthodox theology has grown to take seriously humanity's stewardship over the world. Overpopulation through a lack of control over childbirth is certainly not in keeping with being faithful stewards over our planet and its limited resources. Such issues are particularly acute for churches in countries where overpopulation is a vital issue, such as India or Egypt. For reasons such as these, while there have been some conservative views among the Orthodox Churches that are similar to the stand taken by the Catholics, most of the Orthodox Christian Churches allow contraception within marriage, subject to conditions we will now discuss.

In harmony with their pro-life stance, the Orthodox Churches do ban any form of contraception that involves killing a fetus once it has been conceived.[46] This requires a little explanation. The Church considers human life to begin at the moment of

---

46 For example, the Tenth All-American Council of the Orthodox Church

conception, when the sperm first fertilizes the egg in the mother's Fallopian tube. The reason for this is long and complex, but put as simply as possible, this is the first moment at which a human being has all the genetic information to be the unique individual he or she will grow up to be.

The difference between you as a newly conceived zygote and you today is really just a difference in the number of cells in your body and the complexity of their organization. But from the moment you were conceived, all the information that makes you who you are was right there in that one single fertilized cell; but before it was fertilized, that information wasn't all there. Before conception, neither the egg nor the sperm had the genetic material—and therefore the potential—to become you.

The ancient Church Fathers had different opinions about the moment life begins, as did the scholars of their day, and as do scientists, philosophers, and theologians today, but the Church chooses in such a matter of life and death to err on the side of safety.

This is why abortion is considered a form of murder. By definition, all voluntary abortions are carried out *after* the mother discovers she is pregnant. This usually happens only after a monthly period has been missed, which means that the fetus in her womb is already at least a few weeks old.

By this time the fetus has implanted in the wall of the

---

in America stated in 1992, "Married couples may express their love in sexual union without always intending the conception of a child, but only those means of controlling conception within marriage are acceptable which do not harm a fetus already conceived." The Holy Synod of Bishops, "Synodal Affirmations on Marriage, Family, Sexuality, and the Sanctity of Life," http://oca.org/holy-synod/statements/holy-synod/synodal-affirmations-on-marriage-family-sexuality-and-the-sanctity-of-life, May 2015.

mother's womb and begun to draw nutrition and protection from her. He or she already has a primitive nervous system and a tiny heart that is beginning to beat. Tiny arms and legs have begun to form. Even in its outward shape, the fetus that is aborted is clearly human. The Church therefore condemns abortion in order to protect the rights of the innocent little human life that God has allowed to enter into this world. Once a child has been conceived, it deserves the same right to life as a newborn baby.

Prevention is better than cure, so the Church encourages parents to be diligent in managing their reproductive life, using contraception where necessary to prevent finding themselves in that difficult situation of having an unwanted pregnancy.

However, not all forms of contraception are equal, and the Church accepts some while rejecting others. The guiding principle here is the belief that life begins at conception. Any means of contraception that prevents conception from happening in the first place is acceptable, while any means that has a risk of destroying a living zygote or fetus after conception has occurred is rejected, according to the principles described above.

Using a method of contraception that prevents fertilization is ethically equivalent to abstaining from sex altogether, or to using the rhythm method, both of which are acceptable to the Roman Catholic Church.[47] Whether sex does not occur, or it occurs

---

47 In the rhythm method, the couple engage in sex only during the times of the month when the woman is unlikely to be fertile. In our discussions with members of the Catholic Church, however, there does seem to be some ambiguity as to whether abstinence from sex altogether is the preferred state for Catholic couples who do not wish to have a child. Thus, it is unclear whether, for the Catholic couple, the rhythm method, or "Natural Family Planning," is freely allowed at any time or whether it is meant only to be used in extreme cases of need.

when fertilization is unlikely, or fertilization is prevented by physical or chemical means, the sperm and egg that have been produced simply die and are eliminated from the body. The Orthodox Church treats those situations as being ethically identical in relation to contraception.

In practice, this means that barrier methods (condoms, diaphragms, and so on), spermicidal creams which prevent the sperm from reaching the egg to fertilize it, and the oral contraceptive pill and other delivery methods, such as drug implants under the skin, that prevent conception by various hormonal means, are all acceptable. No fetus is formed that is later destroyed. However, intrauterine devices (IUDs), which can work at least partially by irritating the lining of the womb and preventing a conceived zygote from implanting, and morning-after pills, which have a similar mechanism, are rejected, since they run a significant risk of destroying a living zygote after conception.

Our practice of marriage as an exercise in agape love extends not only to expressing and living such love with our spouses and our born children but even to living it with our unborn children. The pro-life stance of Orthodox Christianity is founded upon this principle of agape love for all human beings. But there are other, less drastic ways of betraying the principle of love that are nonetheless extremely harmful. It is possible, for example, to kill a person's spirit rather than her body.

Domestic Abuse and Violence

Some of the saddest things that can result when people misunderstand the nature and meaning of marriage are abuse and violence. While physical and sexual abuse are almost always inflicted by the man upon the woman, emotional abuse can cut both ways. Emotional abuse can involve using aggression to instill fear in, withhold freedom from, and control the other person. Unfortunately, emotional abuse is often difficult to identify in the absence of other forms of abuse, but it is just as hurtful as any other form. It is of paramount importance that, if you are in a relationship that contains elements of emotional abuse, you seek the assistance of a professional counselor or psychologist. Christian marriages unfortunately are not exempt from this, although it is clearly an abominable and unacceptable betrayal of the kind of agape love we have been talking about.

Abuse is an indication that the abuser sees the victim as something almost less than human, as being more like property over which the abuser has the right to do whatever he wishes, even unto harm. It is no exaggeration to say that abusing another separates a person from Christ and from His Body, the Church. It is a sin of the highest degree because of its unloving nature and because of the horrible consequences that almost always follow from it.

Australian commentator John Dickson recently raised the issue of abuse in Christian marriages in particular in public discussion.[48] He pointed out that churches have sadly and wrongly sometimes allowed abuse to continue through misguidedly encouraging a beaten wife to consider her suffering as "carrying her cross" and to put up with it for the sake of God, her family, and perhaps even her family's reputation.

Such attitudes are thankfully changing, even within more traditional Orthodox Christian communities, and this is certainly a good thing. Abuse of any kind is not something the Church

---

48 See Natasha Moore and John Dickson, "The Church Must Confront Domestic Abuse," http://www.abc.net.au/news/2015-03-12/moore-dickson-the-church-must-confront-domestic-abuse/6300342, April 2015.

should ask people to endure silently but something which the Church must take a stand against and strive to eliminate. Christ was always on the side of the suffering and persecuted, and to allow an abuser to continue to abuse is therefore to put oneself in opposition to Christ. How much more true is this for the abusers themselves?

Abuse can be inflicted on another person in many ways. However, irrespective of the form of abuse, there are some common warning signs that a person may become abusive in the future. The following table outlines a number of questions that will help ascertain the likelihood of abuse either being present now or developing in the future within your relationship.[49] You need to ask yourself these questions in any relationship. If you answer "yes" to any of these questions, then you need to seek professional help for your partner and yourself. These are often early warning signs that your partner is struggling with power and control issues that may lead him to become more abusive as time passes.

Abuse Warning Signs

Inner Thoughts and Feelings	Belittling Behavior
Do you:	Does your partner:
» feel afraid of your partner much of the time?	» humiliate or yell at you?
» avoid certain topics out of fear of angering your partner?	» criticize you and put you down?

---

49   Table adapted from Melinda Smith and Jeanne Segal, "Domestic Violence and Abuse," http://www.helpguide.org/articles/abuse/domestic-violence-and-abuse.htm, April 2015.

» feel that you can't do anything right for your partner?	» treat you so badly that you're embarrassed for your friends or family to see?
» believe that you deserve to be hurt or mistreated?	» ignore or put down your opinions or accomplishments?
» wonder if you're the one who is crazy?	» blame you for his own abusive behavior?
» feel emotionally numb or helpless?	» see you as property or a sex object rather than as a person?
Violent Behavior or Threats	*Controlling Behaviors*
Does your partner:	Does your partner:
» have a bad and unpredictable temper?	» act excessively jealous and possessive?
» hurt you or threaten to hurt or kill you?	» control where you go or what you do?
» threaten to take your children away or harm them?	» keep you from seeing your friends or family?
» threaten to commit suicide if you leave?	» limit your access to money, the phone, or the car?
» force you to have sex or engage in sexual activities?	» constantly check up on you?
» destroy your belongings?	» ask you to keep his behavior secret from your father of confession or other positive influences?

Abusive behavior falls into a common cycle. The cycle usually begins with tensions building between the couple. This tension makes the victim feel afraid, or as if the other partner is unpredictable, and she will try to do anything to bring calm to the relationship. This usually does not work, and the incident of abuse follows. The time between peaks of tension building in a relationship can be as short as minutes or as long as months, but in an abusive relationship it always leads to an incident of abuse.

The abuse can take verbal, emotional, physical, sexual, or other forms, in any combination. Within the incident of abuse, the abuser tends to blame the victim, threaten her, and intimidate her into remaining silent. Once the abuser realizes what he has done, he initiates a reconciliation process filled with apologies, excuses, romantic gestures, promises, and even denial that the incident was as bad as the victim describes it, until calm is restored.

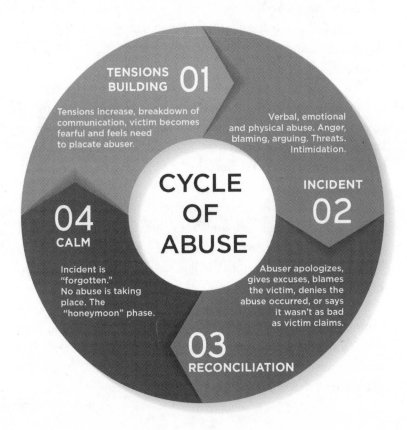

TENSIONS BUILDING 01
Tensions increase, breakdown of communication, victim becomes fearful and feels need to placate abuser.

Verbal, emotional and physical abuse. Anger, blaming, arguing. Threats. Intimidation.

CYCLE OF ABUSE

INCIDENT 02

04 CALM
Incident is "forgotten." No abuse is taking place. The "honeymoon" phase.

Abuser apologizes, gives excuses, blames the victim, denies the abuse occurred, or says it wasn't as bad as victim claims.

03 RECONCILIATION

In most relationships, a period of calm follows after the victim "forgives" the abuser. This is sometimes referred to as a "honeymoon phase," where the relationship seems perfect and the victim starts to feel safe again. This period can last for years in some relationships, or it can be as short-lived as a day. It comes to a bitter end once the tension in the relationship starts to build again. In such a relationship, one person (the victim) is constantly feeling responsible for maintaining the calm in the relationship, as she lives in fear of another abusive incident.

If you are a person who has recognized the early signs of abuse in your relationship prior to marriage, it is imperative that you *do not ignore them*. Most marriages that become abusive had warning signs during engagement that the couple ignored. Such couples were usually still in a romance phase when they married and believed things would get better after marriage.

This is a myth. Abusive patterns tend to become *more* destructive after marriage, not less. While a couple are courting or engaged, the chances of seeking help for both the victim and the abuser are far higher than after marriage, when an abuser may feel that he now "owns" the other partner and will often refuse to seek help.

Unfortunately, one of the early signs of an abusive relationship is that the abuser will demand from the victim that she reveal nothing about the abusive aspects of their relationship to anyone. This is extremely dangerous, as it does not allow the couple to seek objective advice about issues they will face as a couple.

It is important to note that a person who abuses does so as a result of many factors. Such a person will need professional help from a trained counselor or psychologist to navigate through those issues, resolve them, and ultimately learn to partake in healthy relationships. Spiritual guidance is important and valuable, but it does not negate the need for psychological and emotional help from a trained, qualified professional.

As a person might ask a priest to pray for her when she is sick and still seek the advice and medication provided by a doctor, so also for emotional and psychological issues, particularly those relating to abuse. The spiritual and professional approaches work together rather than being mutually exclusive. It is also critically important that *victims* of abuse seek the help of a counselor or psychologist. Victims of abuse often suffer from damaged self-esteem, hurt, and a sense of betrayal. All of these things need to be explored and worked through with a professional, or else they will fester and grow, with harmful and unhappy consequences. In the twenty-first century, and especially in a Christian marriage, no one should have to suffer abuse.

Reflection Questions on Male and Female

» How much does your gender influence your character and behavior? How different do you think your character might be had you been born as a person of the opposite gender?

» How do you see your role as a male or female in your relationship? Do you tend to think in terms of gender role stereotypes, or do you see your role as being defined more by your personality as an individual?

» What are your partner's views on these questions, and how well do your views work together?

» What do you want from your partner in life?

Reflection Questions on Intimacy and Sexuality

» What is the healthy Christian attitude to the body generally and to sexuality in particular, and how does it compare to, say, the attitude of the gnostics?

» What place does sexuality occupy in your character and personality? How important is it in your life? How important is it in your relationship?

» Do you find it easy to talk to your partner about sexual matters? What would make it easier for you to be honest and open?

» What place does unselfish agape love have in a sex life?

» What is the reason for and importance of married couples sometimes abstaining from sex?

Reflection Questions on Contraception and Abortion

» When does life begin?

» How does this understanding influence our attitudes toward contraception and abortion?

» Which forms of contraception are acceptable, and which are not? What is the guiding principle here?

» How do you and your partner feel about having children or about the possibility of delaying having your first child?

Reflection Questions on Domestic Abuse and Violence

» In what ways is abuse in a relationship a betrayal of the Christian principle of agape love?

» What are some of the signs that a relationship is abusive or has the potential to become abusive?

» Is physical violence of any kind ever acceptable in a marriage relationship?

» Why it is important for those involved in an abusive relationship to seek professional help?

CHAPTER SIX

TWO BECOME ONE

Orthodox Marriage Rites

Those whom the Holy Spirit has attuned together
As a stringed instrument, always blessing God
By psalms and hymns and spiritual songs
By day and by night, with an incessant heart.

(GOSPEL RESPONSE,
COPTIC WEDDING CEREMONY)

Holy God, who fashioned man from dust, and from
his rib built up a woman and yoked her to him as
a helper like himself, for it was not pleasing to your
greatness for man to be alone on earth, do you,
Master, now send forth your hand from your holy
dwelling, and link [here the priest joins their right
hands] your servant <name> and your servant
<name> because it is by you that a wife is linked
to her husband. Yoke them together in likeness of
mind. Crown them into one flesh. Grant them fruit
of the womb, enjoyment of fair offspring.

(GREEK ORTHODOX CROWNING SERVICE)

W E WILL CONCLUDE OUR JOURNEY THROUGH engagement and marriage with some descriptions and reflections upon the beautiful rites and rubrics[50] of Orthodox Christian wedding ceremonies. Because all Orthodox Churches share a common apostolic ancestry that reaches back to the age when all Christians were part of one catholic, or universal, Church, their wedding rites share many similarities. We will be discussing the rites of the Coptic and Greek Churches as being representative of the Oriental Orthodox and Eastern Orthodox families, respectively.

It is interesting that, although wedding ceremonies that are separate from the eucharistic Liturgy only developed after the ninth century, some five centuries after the schism at the Council of Chalcedon (AD 451) that split the Eastern Orthodox and Oriental Orthodox families apart, the rites have far more in common than they have differences. To answer the question of why this is would require a fascinating historical study that lies beyond the scope of this book.

When a couple from different Orthodox Churches get engaged or married, there is often an opportunity to have a clergyman from one church attend and participate in the rite in another church. This can only enrich the service, and it is a chance to break down barriers of historical disagreement and misunderstanding, a small grassroots step toward the re-unification of the Churches.

We encourage you, well before your wedding day, to explore together the structure and meaning of your own church's rite. Many parishes offer the opportunity to bring together the families

---

50   A "rubric" in this context is a ritual action performed as part of a religious ceremony—for example, the offering of incense from a censer, or the holding up of a cross.

and the wedding party to meet the priest who will celebrate the wedding and spend some time going through the service with him. This is an excellent opportunity to ask all the questions you like about why things are done and what they mean.

It is only by understanding these profound ancient rites that you can fully participate in the wedding service and experience it as it was meant to be experienced: a spiritual, meaning-laden, and life-transforming encounter with God. You will only get to do this once in your life, so don't let it pass you by in a flurry of smiles at guests and anxieties about flower arrangements!

The Orthodox Marriage Ceremony

The early Church seems not to have had a separate rite for sanctifying marriage, and there was no Byzantine marriage rite separate from the eucharistic Liturgy until the ninth century.[51] There are records, however, of Christian couples having the option (not obligation) of being "crowned" during the eucharistic Liturgy as far back as St. John Chrysostom in the fourth century.[52] For the first half of the Christian era then, marriage was chiefly a civil process that was sanctified and sealed by the couple attending the eucharistic Liturgy together and partaking of Holy Communion together. In this act, they sought Christ Himself to unite them as one.

In the Coptic Church, we find that a church *wedding* ceremony—distinct from the eucharistic Liturgy—was considered compulsory by the Church by at least the thirteenth century,[53]

---

51   See Schmemann, op. cit., p. 88; Meyendorff, op. cit., pp. 24–29.

52   Meyendorff, op. cit., p. 25.

53   Safi Ibn Al-'Assal wrote, "A wedding may be conducted only in the presence of a priest who shall pray for the bridal couple and administer Holy

although the custom was likely to have begun somewhat earlier. As the Coptic rite evolved over the centuries, it expanded to involve the bride and groom attending church on Saturday night to pray and fast together with their families and friends in preparation for the wedding and the liturgy on Sunday morning.

On Sunday morning, after the Morning Raising of Incense, the deacons would first lead the groom into the church in a procession, singing, "O King of Peace" (*Epouro ente ti-hirini*), after which they would lead the bride with her father into the church in a procession, singing, "Hail to Mary" (*Shere Maria*). Once at the front of the church, the groom would receive his bride from the hand of her father, and the marriage ceremony would begin (see details below). Upon its completion, the newly married couple remained in their places at the south side of the royal doors of the sanctuary while the oblations were offered and the liturgy continued. At the end of the liturgy, their marriage was sealed through their receiving Holy Communion side by side, just as in those most ancient times. Thus the first act of their married life together was to be united in Christ by partaking of the Eucharist together.

This is very much in keeping with the ancient Christian understanding of marriage as a "mystery," or a sacrament of the Holy Spirit: "Early Christian writers . . . affirm that it is the Eucharist which gives to marriage its specifically Christian meaning."[54] It is quite rare, but some couples today still choose to be married according to this much longer and more involved rite. The

---

Communion to them in the *iklil* (crown) ceremony, by which they are united and become one flesh, as God Almighty has ordained. Contrary to this it shall not be deemed a proper marriage, for it is through Church prayer alone that man and woman can become mutually legitimate." Quoted in Coptic Encyclopedia, s.v. "marriage."

54 Meyendorff, op. cit., p. 21.

majority, however, prefer to simply have the wedding as a stand-alone ceremony, a rite that takes about one hour to be completed and does not require abstinence from food and drink, as does the eucharistic Liturgy.

The Greek rite also allows for the wedding to be a part of the eucharistic Liturgy, but there too it is relatively rare today, although Meyendorff exhorts, "In our time the connection between marriage and the Eucharist must—and can easily be—restored again."[55] In the modern Roman Catholic rite, both the wedding and the mass are significantly shorter, and neither requires a long period of fasting, so the wedding is routinely performed as part of the mass.

A marriage can be performed any day that is not a fasting day, since the joy and celebration of a wedding are incompatible with the spirit of repentance and spiritual striving during fasting. In the modern Coptic tradition, a wedding may not be performed on the day immediately before a fast begins, although this is not the case in the Greek Church.

The stand-alone ceremony may be performed at any time of the day, since it is not linked to a eucharistic Liturgy, although couples will often attend a liturgy and have communion on the morning before the wedding. If they prefer not to see each other on the morning of their wedding day, they will do so in different parishes. Of course, this is not necessary if the more ancient order is followed and the wedding is itself part of a eucharistic Liturgy. It is, however, advisable for the couple to have confession sometime soon before the wedding so that they may enter their new life together with clean hearts.

As noted above, it is important to remember that marriage is a holy mystery and to plan for the reception party that follows to be

---

55   Op. cit., p. 29.

one that does not take away from that holiness. It makes no sense to celebrate the spiritual unification of the couple by the Holy Spirit by getting drunk or engaging in behaviors that sadden that same Holy Spirit.

In the Coptic Church (but not the Greek), some couples also like to begin their married life after the wedding with a short period of consensual fasting from sexual intercourse (usually one to three days), during which they give themselves to prayer together. This practice emphasizes the authority of the spirit over the desires of the flesh and builds a strong foundation for a life of true, self-sacrificing love for one another and for God. The practice can be found in the Deuterocanonical Book of Tobit (8:4–9).

The Eastern Orthodox ceremony is made up of two services. The first is the betrothal rite, performed in the vestibule or entrance to the church, where the rings are blessed. This represents the "natural" marriage, or a contract of faithfulness between the couple. It was originally a civil ceremony.[56] The prayers remind us that God saved humanity by betrothing it to Himself and that being betrothed to each other is another part of this process of being saved and united with God. The prayers here and in the Coptic ceremony recall the marriages of the patriarchs, Abraham, Isaac, and Jacob. For example, the mission of the servant to find a suitable bride for Isaac among his own people, and the finding and betrothal of Rebecca, reminds us of God's coming to our fallen world to find us and betroth us to His Son, Jesus.

After a solemn procession into the church, the crowning is performed, symbolizing that the couple through marriage are journeying to the Kingdom of heaven, that they are helping

---

56   Op. cit., p. 30.

to establish the Kingdom of God here on earth, and that their self-sacrificial love makes them worthy of the crown of martyr-dom. We will consider some of the profound symbolism and meaning of the rubric of crowning in the next section.

In the Coptic rite, the betrothal or engagement service is per-formed separately at the beginning of the engagement period, while the crowning service marks the transition from the engage-ment period to marriage. Until relatively recently the Coptic wed-ding ceremony service itself comprised two services: the Covenant of the Possessions followed by the Crowning Service. The first ser-vice was formally dropped by decision of the Holy Synod of the Church around the end of the twentieth century, but the crown-ing remains unchanged.

Couples need to be aware of the legal requirements for mar-riage in their civil jurisdiction. In some places, the government appoints the minister of the church as its agent and authorizes him to carry out all the necessary legal paperwork, while in other places a civil marriage is required in addition to the church wed-ding. Some of the paperwork may need to be completed some set period before the wedding ceremony, some of it may take quite some time to go through, and in some places a blood test is legally required. It is important to find out what the requirements are well in advance so you don't miss any deadlines. The parish priest performing the ceremony will generally be able to advise you as to what you need to do and when.

Outline of Two Ceremonies

Below is a brief summary of the more important rites and rubrics of the Orthodox wedding rite. We have room only for a taste of this rich field of study and experience here in this chapter. There is a great deal more that could be said, and indeed a thorough and detailed comparative study of the rites of different Orthodox Churches is waiting for someone to write it. But for our purposes here, we just want to give you and your wedding guests enough material so that you can begin to truly get into the spirit of joy, love, and the presence of God that the Orthodox wedding experience is meant to be.

In researching this section, the authors have been blessed by their exposure to the prayers and rites of a variety of Orthodox Churches, both Eastern and Oriental. Without exception we have found them to be profound spiritual texts full of meaning and significance. Here we can only whet your appetite. We strongly urge you to explore more deeply the prayers and rites of your own church, as this will make your wedding a truly spiritual and life-transforming experience.

Engagement
IN THE COPTIC RITE

Engagement serves the social purpose of formally announcing that a couple are getting to know each other with a view to possible marriage. It is enacted by an exchange of rings, placed by the partners on each other's right ring fingers. This differs from the wedding rite where the priest is the one who places the rings on the fingers (see below). Here, since the couple are the ones who placed the rings, they have the right to remove the rings and break the engagement should things not work out. The exchange of rings may occur just between the families of the couple or with the priest blessing the rings first, either at the home, in a suitable public place, or at church. The priest may pray a simple engagement service. It includes no Bible readings. Usually, a church certificate of engagement is issued.

IN THE GREEK RITE

A blessing of rings is often conducted by the priest in one of the homes of the engaged couple, but there is no separate Church ceremony for engagement as such.

The first part of the marriage ceremony is called the betrothal and was at one time in history performed separately from the crowning service. This is very rare today. Betrothal was never viewed as a "trial period" but as an integral part of the marriage itself, an agreement witnessed by God through the Church. Marrying someone betrothed to another was considered adultery, and breaking a betrothal that had not been sanctified with crowning was considered divorce. In this way it was much more akin to the Jewish tradition of betrothal, whereby St. Mary, although only betrothed to St. Joseph without marriage, was still called his "wife."

Vestments

IN THE COPTIC RITE

The priest wears either the full liturgy vestments or at least the *sadra* (*epitrachelion*, a garment of rich cloth, about 2 meters long and 30 cm wide with an opening for the head, worn so that it reaches down the front to the feet) as a sign of the respect due to an important mystery in which we recognize the divine presence of the Holy Spirit working among us.

IN THE GREEK RITE

The priest wears liturgical vestments with bright colors, most commonly white, signifying the joy of the occasion. The stole (a band of rich cloth about 2–3 meters long and 10 cm wide that is draped around the shoulders) and the chasuble (*phelonion*, a decorated "poncho" worn over the other vestments) are usually worn, the chasuble also signifying joy. Apart from this, there are no rules regarding the priest's vestments.

Surrendering the Bride
IN THE COPTIC RITE

The bride's father brings the bride to the door of the church (or the front of the church),[57] where he surrenders her to the bridegroom. The bridegroom lifts the veil from the bride's face and the priest asks both the bride and the groom to confirm the identity of the other and that they are marrying of their own free will and choice, for marriage must be by the free choice of both partners with no force or coercion involved at all.

The couple are beginning their life as a new independent family and home. The groom thanks the bride's family (represented by the father) for this wonderful gift (his bride) which they have brought into his life.

In the West, marriage is seen as being mainly an agreement between the couple, so the consent is central to the ceremony. In the East (both families of Orthodoxy), marriage is seen primarily as something that is conferred upon the couple by the Church, and so the consent is given a peripheral place in the service.

---

57 The more ancient Coptic rite involves the groom first, then the bride and her father, being led in separate processions to their thrones. This recalls the elaborate ancient Jewish tradition of bringing them in processions all the way from the homes. These Jewish weddings could take up to seven days!

IN THE GREEK RITE

The groom waits outside the church. When the bride arrives, the father hands her over, and the couple enter the church together, led by the priest. While it is popular in Orthodox churches in Western countries for the bridegroom to wait inside the church and the bride to be given away before the altar, this is considered to be non-Orthodox influence.

The bride and groom entering the church together, side by side, may be seen as a symbol of their entering into marriage of their own free will and on equal terms.

In the Slavic rite we find the following questioning of the couple by the officiating priest. It was apparently introduced by Peter Mogila in the seventeenth century.

"Do you, (*name*), have a good, free and unconstrained will and a firm intention to take as your wife (or husband) this woman (or man), (*name*), whom you see here before you? Have you promised yourself to any other bride (or man)?"

Important Hymns
IN THE COPTIC RITE

The hymn *Epouro ente ti-hirini*, "O, King of Peace," normally applied to Christ Himself, is prayed to welcome the groom. The hymn *Shere Maria*, "Hail to Mary," is prayed to welcome the bride.

Jesus Himself is the model of husbandly love, service, self-sacrifice, and peace, through which He showed what true kingship really means. St. Mary is considered our Mother and the spiritual Bride of God (see for instance Song 5:1). She rejoices in the happiness of her children, and she is the perfect model of a pure bride. Thus St. Mary is the model of loving joyful submission to God, a model the bride embraces and imitates in loving her husband. The groom and bride are to take Jesus and Mary as their chief role models and strive to emulate them.

The hymn *Pi-epnevma em-Paracleton*, "The Spirit, the Comforter," is prayed. As the Holy Spirit descended upon the apostles on the day of Pentecost, sanctified them, and united them into the one Body of Christ which is the Church, so we also pray for Him to descend upon this couple and sanctify them, to make them spiritually one, and to make them active members of the Church.

IN THE GREEK RITE

The hymn of Isaiah's Dance is sung: "Rejoice, Isaiah, the Virgin has conceived and has brought forth a son, the Emmanuel, both God and Man: Dayspring is His name. As we magnify Him we call the Virgin Blessed."

This hymn reminds us that marriage and family life play an integral role in our salvation. St. Mary was not only the door by which our Savior entered the world, she also lived the family life with Him. The hymn continues: "Holy Martyrs, who fought the good fight and were crowned, intercede with the Lord to have mercy on our souls."

Like martyrdom, marriage involves a loving self-sacrifice, a commitment to walking in the truth of the faith, and entails a heavenly reward. The crown of marriage is thus in some ways also a crown of spiritual martyrdom.

Sacred Site

IN THE COPTIC RITE

In the Coptic rite, the couple stands in front of thrones set to the south side of the royal doors for most of the service. At the very end, after they have donned capes and crowns and exchanged rings, the curtain of the sanctuary is opened, and they are led around to stand and then kneel before the altar.

The Syriac rite uses a ceremonial table similar to that in the Greek rite.

IN THE GREEK RITE

The rite is performed by a priest who stands before an appropriately covered ceremonial table. It is placed in the middle of the *solea* area of the church, in front of the holy altar.

Upon the table are placed the Holy Gospel, a cup of wine, the betrothal rings, and the wedding crowns. Two candles are lit as a reminder that Christ is "the Light of the world" who offers Himself as illumination for the couple, that they "shall not walk in darkness, but have the light of life" (John 8:12).

The couple stand facing the priest and the royal doors of the holy altar.

Stance of the Couple
IN THE COPTIC RITE

The bride always stands, kneels, walks, or sits at the right hand of the groom. This stems from the words of the psalm: "The queen stood at Your right hand in apparel interwoven with gold, / And adorned and embroidered with various colors" (Ps. 44:10/45:9).

This is the traditional position of strength and honor. For example, we say in the creed that Christ "sits at the right hand of His Father." Also, Eve was taken from Adam's right rib. In this way, the groom honors his bride, expressing his commitment to respect her always and to work in harmony with her as they forge a new life together.

IN THE GREEK RITE

The groom stands to the right of the bride. The right is considered to be preferable to the left (compare the sheep at Christ's right hand at the Second Coming), the position suitable to the one who is to be the "head" of the family. Note that the rings are also placed on the fingers of the right hand.

Candles
IN THE COPTIC RITE

There is no tradition of the couple holding candles, but some couples like to have the flower girl or pageboy hold a candle. Given the length of the service and the danger of fire in the hands of little children, this rarely happens today.

As in all liturgical services, two deacons hold candles on either side of the Gospel as it is being read.

IN THE GREEK RITE

In the Russian rite, candles may be held by the bride and groom throughout the crowning service, representing the lamps of the five wise virgins who were prepared for and welcomed Christ the Bridegroom. This is rare in the Greek rite but not unheard of.[58]

Blessing the Rings
IN THE COPTIC RITE

The rings are tied together with a red ribbon or white kerchief and blessed three times in the name of the Father, the Son, and the Holy Spirit. The red ribbon represents the blood of our Lord

---

58 For example, Fr. Anthony Coniaris mentions it in his 1972 booklet, *Getting Ready for Marriage in the Orthodox Church* (Brookline: Light and Life Publishing), perhaps because this booklet was intended for a pan-Orthodox readership rather than just for the Greek Church.

Jesus Christ by which we were saved, and by His grace we received the mystery of marriage, in which the Holy Trinity unites the two individuals into one. This is a reminder of the role that marriage plays in our salvation and of its representing the relationship between God and humanity. The couple are reminded to follow the example of Christ, who loved His spouse, the Church, and shed His blood and gave His life for her.

A white kerchief indicates the purity and holiness of the mystery of marriage.

IN THE GREEK RITE

In the vestibule, the priest takes the rings and with them makes the sign of the cross on the forehead of the groom, saying three times: "The servant of God (*groom*) is betrothed to the servant of God (*bride*) in the name of the Father, and of the Son, and of the Holy Spirit. Amen."

The same procedure is repeated, making the sign of the cross over the bride's forehead, signifying the equality of man and woman in the eyes of God. At the conclusion, the rings are placed on the fourth finger of the right hands of the couple.

The *paranymphos* or *koumbaros* (the best man) steps forward and, crossing his hands first, takes the rings and exchanges them, over and under, on the same fingers, three times.

The priest then recites a prayer beseeching God "to bless this putting on of rings with a heavenly blessing and that an angel of the Lord will go before these Your servants, all the days of their life." Here ends the betrothal service.

Rings

IN THE COPTIC RITE

The rings are symbolic of many things. They are made of gold that does not rust or become corrupted in any way, as marriage is a mystery beyond price, holy, pure, and incorruptible by the world, when the couple maintain its sanctity.

The rings are round—without beginning and without end—as the mystery of marriage is an eternal bond[59] and an icon of the eternal marriage of the Church to her Groom, Christ. The rings have the name of the spouse engraved on them as a sign that the two are now one, that their lives belong to one another, and that each is the precious ornament of the other. They are placed on the left ring finger, since the left side is nearest to the heart. And finally, they are placed on the fingers of the couple by the priest (representing the Church) as a sign that the Church alone can remove them, since "what God has joined together, let not man separate" (Matt. 19:6).

IN THE GREEK RITE

The rings are a sign of the covenant of faithfulness between the couple. The prayers of the betrothal service mention four biblical examples of rings binding people together: Pharaoh and Joseph (Gen. 41:42); the ring that saved Tamar from Judah (Gen. 38:1–26); King Darius sealing Daniel in the lion's den with his ring, in hope of his deliverance (Dan. 6:17–19); and the ring the joyous father gave his returned prodigal son (Luke 15:22).

---

59 For a detailed discussion of differing Christian views on whether marriage continues beyond death, see Meyendorff, op. cit., pp. 12–16. His conclusion is, "Christian marriage is not only an earthly sexual union, but an eternal bond which will continue when our bodies will be 'spiritual' and when Christ will be 'all in all.'" Op. cit., p. 15.

The rings are placed on the right hand in memory of the right hand of Moses, which he stretched out over the waters of the Red Sea to make them fall back upon Pharaoh's army, thus delivering the Israelites to safety (Ex. 14:26). So also through this mystery the couple are delivered from the raging ocean of this fallen world.

Holding Hands

IN THE COPTIC RITE

Once the rings are in place, the couple's hands are joined together and covered with a white kerchief. They remain so to the end of the ceremony. This signifies that, through marriage, the two have become one flesh, and the pure white kerchief signifies the Holy Spirit overshadowing them and uniting them as one.

IN THE GREEK RITE

The priest then beseeches God "to unite the bridal couple in concord and crown them in one flesh." At this point the right hands of the bride and groom are joined by the priest. They remain joined throughout the remainder of the Service, symbolizing the oneness of the couple.

Capes

IN THE COPTIC RITE

After a prayer of blessing, a cape, or *bornos*, is placed on the couple's shoulders. The cape is a royal and priestly garment. The groom is becoming the "king" and the "priest" of the family. He is responsible for their spiritual growth and development. The bride wears a smaller cape,[60] signifying that she shares this

---

60   While the tradition of the groom's cape goes back centuries, the bride's cape is an interesting recent addition that was introduced in the first years of the twenty-first century, perhaps in acknowledgement of the

responsibility with her husband, being the "queen" of the new family and working together in synergy with her husband for the spiritual welfare of the whole home. As they are to sanctify the little part of the world that is their home, they are contributing to the sanctification of the whole world, which is the priestly service of Christ, in whose image they are.

IN THE GREEK RITE

There is no donning of capes.

Anointing with Oil

IN THE COPTIC RITE

After a prayer of blessing, the couple are anointed with oil, each on the forehead, upper chest or neck, and the two wrists. Anointment with oil generally symbolizes the work of the Holy Spirit in our lives. Here we pray to the Holy Spirit that He may sanctify, purify, and strengthen the couple's mind (anointing the forehead), heart (anointing the upper chest), and actions (anointing the wrists). It is also a symbol of joy—our joy over the couple being united in marriage, as well as a prayer for God to fill their lives with His joy.

IN THE GREEK RITE

There is no anointing with oil.

Incense

IN THE COPTIC RITE

Incense is offered as in most liturgical services to remind us of the sacrifice of Christ, who gave Himself up as a sweet aroma

---

more equal balance of responsibility between husbands and wives that characterizes modern society gender roles.

of salvation that spread throughout the whole world. We are reminded that marriage is a part of this process of salvation and that, by seeking to be Christlike in love, the couple are finding their own salvation and sharing the Gospel of salvation with everyone around them. In living a life together of such self-sacrificial love, they too, like Christ, will become a sweet aroma to all around them.

IN THE GREEK RITE
The Greek rite does not include the offering of incense.

Crowns
IN THE COPTIC RITE
Two crowns are blessed and then placed on the couple's heads. These represent the authority of the bride and groom over their new household. They symbolize their authority to have self-control and to live a pure and holy life. They are crowns of victory over the unbridled passions of the flesh, taming them and sanctifying them under the rule of agape love. They are also the heavenly crowns awaiting those who live their lives in purity and holiness (2 Tim. 4:7–8; see also St. John Chrysostom, *Homilies on 2 Timothy*, Homily 9). Thus they are circular, reminding us of the eternity of God's love for us and of our love for one another.

The bride and groom are also crowns for one another (see Prov. 12:4; 1 Cor. 11:3), and they become each other's "crown and glory." They are also crowns of martyrdom, in both senses of the word: the couple are called to be martyrs (witnesses) of the truth of the Gospel with their lives of unconditional love, and they are also called to be martyrs (give up their lives) for each other through constant self-giving and sacrifice.

Lastly, when the groom looks to his crowned bride and sees a queen before him, he pledges his undying loyalty and love to her and in his heart offers to her his life for her service forevermore. Likewise, when the bride looks to her crowned husband, she sees a king before her and likewise pledges her life to him forever.

IN THE GREEK RITE

The crowning ceremony is the climax of the marriage service. In the Orthodox Church, each wedding is a form of coronation service. Since the bride and groom are regarded as part of the "royal family" of God, they are crowned king and queen of their own dominion—their new fellowship and family. Crowns are a symbol of victory for those who "have fought the good fight" of the Christian life and "have kept the faith" (2 Tim. 4:7). In short, both they and the actual office of marriage are given great honor. The crowns were usually plaited of lemon blossoms or flowers. Today they are often made of silver or gold. They are a sign of the bond between the bride and groom and represent the glory and honor that God bestows upon the couple who have observed His commandments.

The most beautiful and significant symbolism of the crown is expressed in the words of the priest before placing them on the couple. Making the sign of the cross on the groom's forehead, he exclaims three times, "The servant of God (*groom*) takes as his crown the servant of God (*bride*) in the name of the Father and of the Son and of the Holy Spirit. Amen."

Similarly, signifying equality once again and making the sign of the cross on the bride's forehead, the priest exclaims three times, "The servant of God (*bride*) takes as her crown the servant of God (*groom*) in the name of the Father and of the Son and of the Holy Spirit. Amen."

These words indicate that the great crown in marriage—your

great glory—is the one you have chosen to be joined to for the rest of your life.

The best man then exchanges the crowns three times while the priest and the chanter sing, "Lord our God, crown them in glory and honor."

Symbols of Unity in Love
IN THE COPTIC RITE

The couple lean over sideways, bring their heads together till they touch, and are blessed three times in the name of the Holy Trinity by the priest. Leaning over symbolizes that, to be united in love and humility, they have to meet each other halfway. The triple blessing expresses the spiritual mystery of the couple being drawn into the circle of love of the Holy Trinity. In His great love for us, God shares the love that is between the Father, the Son, and the Holy Spirit by adopting us—and today, especially the couple—and including us in that love.

IN THE GREEK RITE

The crowns placed on the heads of the couple are tied together, connected by a single ribbon of rich material. This symbolizes the unity of their thought and spirit and that they must win their heavenly crown of salvation together, not alone.

The sense of unity in Christ is also signified by the holding of hands and by their drinking from the common cup.

Readings
IN THE COPTIC RITE

The readings come before the crowning, which is the "crown" or climax of the ceremony. The Pauline epistle is Ephesians 5:22–6:3; the psalm is from Psalms 18:6–7/19:5–6 and 127/128:3–4:

"And it rejoices exceedingly / Like a bridegroom coming forth from his bridal chamber, / Like a strong man to run a race . . . Your wife shall be like a vine, prospering on the sides of your house; / Your children like newly planted olive trees / Around your table." The Gospel is Matthew 19:1–6, ending: "So then they are no longer two but one flesh. Therefore what God has joined together, let not man separate."

IN THE GREEK RITE

With the crowns now placed on the heads of the bride and groom uniting them as husband and wife, the epistle is read from St. Paul's Letter to the Ephesians (5:20–33). The Gospel is then read from John (2:1–11, the wedding at Cana of Galilee).

Before the Altar of God
IN THE COPTIC RITE

The couple kneel before the open royal sanctuary door (before the altar) side by side while the priest reads to them the exhortations (advice on how to have a successful married life). They kneel with royal crowns on their heads before the royal doors of the altar, the throne of Christ. Their royalty and nobility of character are derived from His. Kneeling is a sign of the submission and surrender of their whole lives to God. As part of their submission to God, the couple are also commanded by Him to submit to one another in love, joy, and humility.

IN THE GREEK RITE

The couple stand before the small table placed outside the sanctuary, bearing the Gospel, the crowns, the rings, and the cup of wine.

Toward the end of the ceremony the priest removes the crowns from the couple's heads and replaces them on this table, praying, "Take up their crowns in your Kingdom, unspotted and unblemished, and keep them without offence to the ages of ages." This represents the couple, offering their life together wholly to God, through the intercession of the Church.

The Common Cup
IN THE COPTIC RITE

There is no common cup within the Coptic marriage ceremony itself, but traditionally the wedding took place before the eucharistic liturgy (see above). After the wedding ceremony, the first act the couple performs in their life together is to attend the liturgy and partake of Holy Communion together.

IN THE GREEK RITE

That Jesus chose a wedding to enact his first miracle is the most profound indication of the dignity attributed to the union of man and woman by God. Since the changing of water into wine at Cana, Jesus continues to change the "water" of ordinary relationships into the "wine" of sacramental marriage. In remembrance of Christ's first miracle, therefore, the bride and groom share a communal cup of wine as a sign of unity with each other and with Christ.

This is not Holy Communion. Rather, it is a symbol of the "common cup of life," a sign denoting the mutual sharing of joy and sorrow, a token of harmony. The priest offers the cup first to the groom and then to the bride.

The Dance of Isaiah
IN THE COPTIC RITE

The Coptic rite does not include this procession, although it has a less formal procession—after the crowning, the priest opens the curtain of the sanctuary and then leads the couple from their thrones at the south of the chancel to stand facing east before the altar.

IN THE GREEK RITE

The procession, a symbolic liturgical dance for the joy of God's presence, is conducted in a circular fashion (reminding us of the eternity of love) with the Holy Gospel in the hands of the priest, who leads the couple while holding their united hands. This highlights the Church's prayerful desire that the couple will walk through life led by the infallible and secure Word of God and inspired by the Church.

During the procession, the priest and the chanter sing the hymn, "Rejoice,[61] Isaiah, the Virgin has conceived and has brought forth a son, the Emmanuel, both God and Man: Dayspring is His name. As we magnify Him we call the Virgin Blessed." The second and third hymns remind the newlyweds of the virtuous lives of the saints and martyrs whose faith and sacrifice they are called to emulate.

Exhortation
IN THE COPTIC RITE

The priest reads out the exhortations (sometimes translated "commandments") to the bride and groom as they stand side by side before the open sanctuary and altar (see also below). They are

---

61 Literally, *choreue*, a call to perform a *chorodia*, a triple circular procession known in both ancient Jewish and Greek tradition.

advised to keep God always in their midst, to respect and obey each other, and to bring joy into each other's lives.

IN THE GREEK RITE

There are blessings rather than advice. The priest says to the groom, "Bridegroom, be magnified like Abraham, blessed like Isaac, and multiplied like Jacob, as you go your way in peace and carry out in righteousness the commandments of God." To the bride he says, "And you, Bride, be magnified like Sarah, and rejoice like Rebecca, and be multiplied like Rachel, rejoicing in your own husband, keeping the limits of the law, for so God has been well-pleased."

Absolution
IN THE COPTIC RITE

The couple kneel together in humility before the altar while the priest prays the absolution of sins for them, the same absolution used in the mystery of Confession. The priest crosses his hands over the couple's heads as he prays, signifying that from now on their hitherto individual searches for salvation in Christ are intertwined indissolubly together as one.

Through the grace of this sacrament, all the sins of their past are absolved and forgiven, and they start their life together with completely pure hearts.

When the prayers conclude, the priest removes the crowns and the capes.

IN THE GREEK RITE

Following the procession, the priest places his hand on the couple's heads, first the groom's and then the bride's, and speaks over each the appropriate blessing, as described above.

During the ensuing prayer, the priest removes the crowns from the newlyweds' heads, praying, "O God, our God, who when You were present in Cana of Galilee blessed the marriage there, bless also these Your servants who have been joined together by Your providence in the fellowship of marriage; bless their comings in and their goings out; make their lives fruitful for good; take their crowns unto Your kingdom and preserve them blameless, guileless, and unstained unto the ages of ages. Amen."

In the past, the couple would wear their crowns for eight days before having them removed by the priest.

Conclusion
IN THE COPTIC RITE

The service ends with the usual concluding hymn and benediction. The newly married couple are then led out of the church by the choir in a joyous procession.

IN THE GREEK RITE

The service closes with the benediction, "Through the prayers of our Holy Fathers have mercy upon us, Lord Jesus Christ our God, and save us. Amen." Before congratulating the newlyweds, the priest takes the Holy Gospel and separates their right hands with it, thus signifying that nothing and no one, except God alone, who forgives and unites and strengthens, should come between the new couple.

The Coptic Orthodox explanation above is based on The Sacraments of the Church vol. 6: Holy Matrimony *by His Grace Bishop Mettaous (Mariut, Egypt: St. Mina Monastery Press, 2000), and* Understanding:

Year 12 Coptic Orthodox Studies Textbook (*Coptic Orthodox Church, Diocese of Sydney and Affiliated Regions*, 3rd edition, 2008).

The Greek Orthodox explanation above is based on The Sacrament of Marriage According to the Rites of The Greek Orthodox Church, available from the official website of the Greek Orthodox Archdiocese of Australia: *http://www.greekorthodox.org.au/general/resources/service-booklets/wedding* accessed April 2015, and on personal communication with Fr. Vassilios Papavassiliou.

Various other explanations are from Marriage: An Orthodox Perspective, by Fr. John Meyendorff (see bibliography).

ROLE PLAY WITH TRANSLATIONS

Rupert & Cynthia Have an Argument

What they SAY.

What they really MEAN.

[Rupert walks in cheerfully, holding flowers behind his back.]

RUPERT:

Hi dear! Sorry I'm late—I got held up at the office by that new Japanese client. Never seen anyone who cares so much about details! It was, "this is too small," and, "that's too red," and, "you didn't put enough of this in." I'd hate to be his wife, hey! Anyway, look. I'm really sorry, and I just got you a little something to show you how sorry I am . . .

[Proudly, he produces flowers from behind his back. Cynthia looks at him coldly and turns away without taking the flowers. Rupert continues, less certain of himself.]

I love you.
You are so important to me.

RUPERT:

I, er . . . I had a lot of trouble choosing these, you know.

What am I doing wrong?

Ummmm. You don't like them?

CYNTHIA:

Rupert, sometimes I wonder if
you still love me . . .

I am stressed and lonely.
I need reassurance.

RUPERT:

Love you? Of course I love you,
you silly woman! What do you
think these flowers are for?

You are everything to me!
*Rupert has taken Cynthia's words
literally and found them illogical.
Big mistake.*

CYNTHIA:

You never spend time with me
anymore.

I miss you. I enjoy your company,
and I need more time with you.
But I don't want to come across
as needy.

RUPERT:

What??? Come on, last Tuesday
we had a lovely evening together.

But I am trying so hard. I am
frustrated that it isn't working.
Why I can't I get this right?
*Rupert has interpreted Cynthia's
words literally again, totally missing the point. All Cynthia hears
from Rupert's words is, "You're
stupid and ungrateful. You can't
even remember the kind things I
do for you."*

CYNTHIA:

[giving a withering stare] Most
of the time, it's as if I'm not even
there. You just ignore me. You're
too tied up with your stupid job
and your stupid Chinese friend.

I'm uncertain where I am in your
life. Am I still important to you?
*Cynthia is totally missing the
uncertainty and despair that's
growing inside Rupert.*

RUPERT:

Number one, he's not my friend, he's a client—he pays for our life-style. And number two, he's not Chinese, he's Japanese. And—

By continuing to miss Cynthia's point, Rupert is only frustrating her more and making her feel unloved and alone.

CYNTHIA:

[*cutting him off angrily*] I don't care if he's an Eskimo from Afghanistan—you don't love me the way you used to!

Why don't you get what I am trying to tell you?
Why can't I make you understand?
Please reassure me that I am still important to you.

RUPERT:

I don't . . . What do you mean . . . Oh, I give up. This is pointless.

[Rupert turns and walks over to a chair, sits down and switches on the TV using a remote. His eyes are glued to the TV as the conversation continues.]

This is just too hard for me. I feel a little sorry for myself. This is so unfair.
Men need to feel in control of a situation. When they aren't, they just want to escape the situation and go back into their caves until they work it out.

CYNTHIA:

What do you think you're doing? You're not going to watch TV now?

I need to talk to you so I can feel better.

RUPERT:

Come on Cynthia, I'm tired and I really don't want to get into this now. We can sort it out tomorrow.

If you let me calm myself down a little first and think things through, I will be better able to give you what you need.

CYNTHIA:
You're upset with me, aren't you?

I am afraid I am losing you.

RUPERT:
I'm not upset, I'm OK.

I'm upset with myself. I should have handled this better.

CYNTHIA:
Yes you are. You're just switching off.

All Rupert hears is, "You're running away like a baby. You're not clever enough to fix this."

RUPERT:
Look, I'm not upset. It's not a problem.

Please, just give me some space, and I will find a solution and make you happy again.

CYNTHIA:
Not a problem? Not a problem??? You don't think we have a problem?

You're denying my feelings as if they weren't important. You're denying your own feelings as if they don't exist.

RUPERT:
I didn't say . . .

The last thing I want to do is hurt you. Please let me clarify what I meant.

CYNTHIA:
[cutting him off] How can you do this? How can you sit there and say we have no problem? Why do you think I'm upset? Why do you think you're so upset with me?

Oh no! I was right! He doesn't care about me. I have lost his interest and maybe even his love. If he cared, he would be as upset as I am.

RUPERT:
Look, for the last time, I'm NOT upset. I'm fine. Now just leave me

Why can't you understand? I can't make you feel better

alone or I WILL get upset!
[An extremely tense minute passes]

RUPERT:
[taking his eyes off the TV at last]
Come and sit down.
[She sits next to him.] Don't you
know you're the most important
thing in my whole life? Don't you
know that making you happy is
what matters the most to me? It's
just that sometimes I don't know
what to do to make you happy,
and I make mistakes. You've gotta
help me out.

CYNTHIA:
Look, I'm sorry, Rupert. I know
you've had a hard day. I really
appreciate how hard you work for
us both. And I really appreciate
that you went out of your way to
get those flowers for me. You're a
good husband. But if I don't blow
off steam with you, who can I
blow it off with? My mother?

when I feel like a failure.

*Finally, he is expressing his feel-
ings. Cynthia needed to know that
he still cares enough about her to
have these feelings.*

*Finally, she is acknowledging his
efforts and his successes, making
him feel less like a failure, thus
enabling him to care for her again.*

Select Bibliography

Below are some books you may find helpful should you wish to explore further any of the topics covered in this book.

Marriage Rites

Greek Orthodox Archdiocese of America, "The Service of the Crowning—The Service of Marriage," http://www.goarch.org/chapel/liturgical_texts/wedding
See also http://www.anastasis.org.uk/betrotha.htm (betrothal) and www.anastasis.org.uk/crowning.htm (crowning).
The text of the Greek Orthodox wedding rite.

Kaldas, Fr. Antonios, "Marriage Ceremony According to the Coptic Orthodox Rite—with Explanations," http://wp.me/PH9eM-e4
The text of the Coptic Orthodox wedding rite, complete with explanatory annotations. Click the link you find near the top of the page to download. Couples may insert their names into the text and print it for the use of their guests or screen it in the church during the ceremony.

Theology of Marriage

Coptic Encyclopedia, (Claremont: Claremont Graduate University School of Religion, 1991), s.v. "marriage."

Available online at Bishop Gregorius, "Marriage," http://ccdl.libraries.claremont.edu/cdm/singleitem/collection/cce/id/1285/rec/1
An overview of the scriptural basis, theology, and history of marriage and the marriage ceremony in the Coptic Orthodox Church. Another entry, "Marriage Customs," by Cérès Wissa Wassef in the same encyclopedia, features some fascinating popular customs. Most of these are no longer practiced by

Copts, at least in urban Egypt and the diaspora, although some survive in rural Egypt.

Farley, Lawrence R., *One Flesh: Salvation through Marriage in the Orthodox Church* (Chesterton, IN: Ancient Faith Publishing, 2013).
Historical and theological treatment of marriage.

Bishop Mettaous, *The Sacraments of the Church vol. 6: Holy Matrimony* (Mariut, Egypt: St. Mina Monastery Press, 2000).
A very basic outline of the Coptic Orthodox understanding of the sacrament of marriage by a highly respected Coptic Church authority on rites and traditions. For those interested in recent developments, though, the essay titled "Sacraments and Symbol," in Schmemann's For the Life of the World, *gives a fascinating critique of this kind of approach and its relation to authentic ancient Christianity.*

Meyendorff, Fr. John, *Marriage: An Orthodox Perspective* (Crestwood, NY: St. Vladimir's Seminary Press, 1984).
Eastern Orthodox scholar Meyendorff looks at marriage against the background of Judaism, the New Testament, the early Church, Roman law, and contemporary life. Covers issues including second marriage, mixed marriage, divorce, abortion, family planning, responsible parenthood, and more.

Schmemann, Fr. Alexander, "The Mystery of Love," in *For the Life of the World* (Crestwood, NY: SVS Press, 1973).
This Eastern Orthodox modern classic looks at the sacramental life of Orthodox Christianity. Chapter 5 is dedicated to the mystery of marriage. Why should we consider marriage a sacrament, and what does that actually mean? As usual, his criticisms of certain aspects of modern Christian approaches to marriage are just as illuminating and interesting as his positive reflections.

Ancient Fathers on Marriage

St. John Chrysostom, *On Marriage and Family Life*, trans. Catherine
P. Roth and David Anderson (Crestwood, NY: SVS Press,
1986).
*Selections from the homilies of St. John Chrysostom that
relate to marriage and family life in an accessible translation.
It is astonishing how relevant this fifth-century wisdom is to
twenty-first–century life!*

Wahba, Fr. Matthias F., *Honorable Marriage According to St. Athanasius* (Brookline, MA: Light & Life Publishing, 1996).
*An in-depth and very carefully researched account of views on
marriage from pre-Christian times, through the early Church,
and up to the views of the highly influential St. Athanasius in
the fourth century.*

Married Life

Chapman, Gary, *The Five Love Languages* (Chicago: Northfield Publishing, 1995).
*The popular text that helps you to identify your chief "love lan-
guage"—how you best experience and give love—as well as that
of your partner. Very helpful for making sure you communicate
love effectively.*

Coniaris, Fr. Anthony, *Getting Ready for Marriage in the Orthodox
Church* (Brookline, MA: Light & Life Publishing, 1972).
*A short booklet with lots of practical advice on preparing for a
wedding, married life, and the wedding ceremony itself. A little
dated in places, but very useful.*

Edelman, Sarah, *Change Your Thinking* (Sydney: ABC Books, 2006).
*A very practical, easy to read and apply guide to using cognitive
behavioral techniques to change how you think and act and to
help you have a more healthy and positive attitude to life.*

Gray, John, *Men are from Mars, Women are from Venus* (New York: HarperCollins, 2003).
>
> *The popular text that describes the differences in the communication and coping styles of men and women and gives advice on how the two can live together in peace and harmony.*

Holly, Fr. Dn. Stephen, *How Do I Choose the Right Partner for Life?* (Brookline: Light & Life Publishing, 2003).
>
> *A short booklet with much pastoral wisdom behind it and lots of good advice on how to go about making the right decision.*

Joanides, Charles, *Attending Your Marriage: A Resource for Christian Couples* (Brookline: Light & Life Publishing, 2006).
>
> *This book is mostly about fixing a bad marriage relationship.*

Keirsey, David and Marilyn Bates, *Please Understand Me* (Del Mar: Prometheus Nemesis Book Company, 1984).
>
> *An application of the widely used Myers-Briggs Personality Scale to relationships. Find out which of the 16 types you are and which one best fits your spouse, and learn to appreciate the differences and use them to your mutual benefit.*

Littauer, Florence, *Personality Plus for Couples* (Ada, MI: Baker Publishing Group, 2001).
>
> *A book about what to expect of yourself and your spouse based on your personality type. It includes a simple personality test and pages of stories and practical insights about how to approach each kind of personality differently.*

Mason, Mike, *The Mystery of Marriage: As Iron Sharpens Iron* (Colorado Springs: Multnomah Press, 1985).
>
> *A beautifully written contemplation on the spiritual aspects of married life by a Protestant author.*

About the Authors

IRENI ATTIA is a Christian counselor who has been working in private practice in Sydney, Australia, since 2005, as well as being a school counselor since 2010. She works with individuals, couples, families, and groups, addressing a range of issues. She enjoys facilitating parenting and relationship seminars with the aim of helping couples and families establish and maintain healthy relationships. She is married with two children.

FR. ANTONIOS KALDAS has served as parish priest of Archangel Michael and St. Bishoy Coptic Orthodox Church in Mount Druitt, Sydney, Australia, since 1991. He was previously a medical doctor, has been heavily involved in the spiritual education of children and youth, is currently an active researcher in the philosophy of mind and cognitive science at Macquarie University, and lectures in apologetics and philosophy at St. Cyril's Coptic Orthodox Theological College (formerly Pope Shenouda III Theological College) in Sydney. He is married with two children and a number of pets.

Also from Ancient Faith Publishing

Parenting Toward the Kingdom:
Orthodox Christian Principles of Child-Rearing

by Philip Mamalakis, PhD

The Orthodox Christian tradition is filled with wisdom and guidance about the biblical path of salvation. Yet this guidance remains largely inaccessible to parents and often disconnected from the parenting challenges we face in our homes. *Parenting Toward the Kingdom* will help you make the connections between the spiritual life as we understand it in the Orthodox Church and the ongoing challenges of raising children. It takes the best child development research and connects it with the timeless truths of our Christian faith to offer you real strategies for navigating the challenges of daily life.

Blueprints for the Little Church:
Creating an Orthodox Home

by Elissa D. Bjeletich and Caleb Shoemaker

How do we as Orthodox parents keep our children in the Church throughout their lives? It all begins with involving them in the life of the Church from birth onward—in the parish and also at home. *Blueprints for the Little Church* provides practical ideas and encouragement—without judgment—for incorporating the primary practices of Orthodox spirituality into your family life at every stage of its growth and throughout the church year.

We hope you have enjoyed and benefited from this book. Your financial support makes it possible to continue our nonprofit ministry both in print and online. Because the proceeds from our book sales only partially cover the costs of operating **Ancient Faith Publishing** and **Ancient Faith Radio**, we greatly appreciate the generosity of our readers and listeners. Donations are tax deductible and can be made at **www.ancientfaith.com**.

To view our other publications,
please visit our website: **store.ancientfaith.com**

 **ANCIENT FAITH RADIO**

Bringing you Orthodox Christian music, readings,
prayers, teaching, and podcasts 24 hours a day since 2004 at
www.ancientfaith.com